The Ultimate Yorkshire Terrier Book

Guide to Caring, Raising, Training, Breeding, Whelping, Feeding and Loving a Yorkie

by
Patricia O'Grady

authorHOUSE®

AuthorHouse™
1663 Liberty Drive
Bloomington, IN 47403
www.authorhouse.com
Phone: 1-800-839-8640

First published by AuthorHouse   12/7/2009

ISBN: 978-1-4490-4385-8 (e)
ISBN: 978-1-4490-4384-1 (sc)
ISBN: 978-1-4490-5136-5 (hc)

Library of Congress Control Number: 2009912334

Printed in the United States of America
Bloomington, Indiana

This book is printed on acid-free paper.

I dedicate this book with love and appreciation, to my parents for all the reasons they know so well. I love you both, always and forever.

A special note to Hope, Love and Faith, I know that all dogs go to heaven, because there could be no place else that such pure love could go. I will see you again, wait for me at the Rainbow Bridge.

THE YORKSHIRE TERRIER

People love dogs
Of every size and hue,
But my favorite by far is the one
That sports a hair coat of tan and blue.

Prancing little show dogs
Their hair flows in a mane
Grooming them is a hassle,
Sometimes a big pain.

The Yorkie protects it territory,
With eyes beaming bright,
So God help any cat or squirrel,
That happens to come into sight.

Affectionate by nature
Some can't control their licker,
That tiny little tongue,
Will come at you in a flicker.

They usually wear a hair bow
In colors of pink, red or blue,
It seriously doesn't bother them,
They honestly have no clue.

They have a long silky coat,
It's your job to daily brush,
They seem to enjoy this attention,
So don't be in a rush.

They can be picky eaters
Rarely finish their food
Take care preparing their meals
They eat depending on their mood.

These tiny little creatures
With pricked up ears,
Make wonderful watchdogs,
And will bark at everything it hears.

When the long day is over
And you lay down your head,
You should expect to find this dog
Cuddled up in your bed.

"To those who claim that money can't buy love or happiness, I say they forgot about Yorkie puppies"

Table of Contents

The Delightful Yorkshire Terrier

The Yorkshire Terrier has a diminutive size, long silky coat and delightful facial expression. If you want a dog that is affectionate, small, elegant, easy to carry and doesn't take up much space, than a Yorkshire Terrier is your dog. If you are looking for a low maintenance breed, than you need to pass, because they do require much attention and grooming. They are lively and inquisitive and have a unmistakable spunky character. The breed is often affectionately called "Yorkie" as a nickname, and you'll soon see that they to have big personalities despite their petite size.

You can expect your Yorkie to be fearless, determined, full of energy, loveable and sometimes rather stubborn. Not surprisingly Yorkshire Terriers are the 2nd most popular dog in the United States having been listed in the top 10 of most popular owned breeds for many years. In case you are curious, the Labrador Retriever is currently listed as number one.

Don't let their tiny stature fool you, they are surprisingly courageous, and can make an excellent watchdog. Since they have a great sense of hearing, they will usually hear someone approaching, long before they even get to opportunity to ring the doorbell. A word of warning though, they can become chronic yappers, if they are not properly trained. You must make them understand barking at just everything and anything is not acceptable behavior. You will need to be verbally strong with them, because they are so cute and small in size, many owners tend to allow them to get away with behaviors that other dogs would not, making the Yorkie believe that it is pack leader, when the owner should be in charge, and assume that position. You must show them leadership, gently, never physically striking them, but verbally firm, so that your puppy understands you are in charge before negative behaviors begin.

They are perfect for apartment living or homes that just don't have a lot of space, as they require limited room for exercise. Yorkies delight in cuddling on your lap, being primped, loved and petted. They are extremely devoted to their owners. Most will prefer to share your bed if you allow it.

Yorkshire Terriers are easy recognized by their long luxurious silky blue and tan coats, usually wearing a hair ribbon on their topknot. It's not uncommon today, to see Yorkies sporting dresses or shirts, as the dog industry seems to understand our love for the little darlings, many people treat them like children rather than dogs. Some Yorkies seem to enjoy being dressed in clothing, and will prance around to show off a new outfit. They prefer warmer weather, so if you do live in a colder environment, a good sweater or dog coat is recommended.

Yorkshire Terriers are a portable size pooch and travel well, and delight in the attention they receive when visiting outside of the home. They make wonderful pets and will easily adapt to most homes.

I have often told others, that once you own a Yorkie you will never own another breed. Many Yorkie owners have more than one, because caring for two isn't much more work than caring for one, and Yorkies enjoy the company of their own. I have spent many hours being entertained just watching my own dogs interact with each other it can be quite amusing. Owning more than one also eases my guilt when I go out to run errands, because I know they have each other's company while I am gone. Make no mistake, yorkies have a great need for interaction with their owners, and always want to please. This breed can suffer from separation anxiety more than some of the other breeds, and requires a great deal of human companionship. They dislike being left alone for more than a few hours, so if you work all day, this is probably not the best breed for you, unless you are able to stop home during your lunch hour to reassure your dog. You can always expect your Yorkie to greet you at the door, welcoming your arrival back home.

The Origin of the Yorkshire Terrier

Named after the city from which they originally hail, Yorkshire Terriers were bred in Yorkshire, Northern England in the 1800's. This glamorous fashion breed didn't start out that way; they were bred for the purposes of hunting and killing rats. In the early 19th century Yorkies were carried in the pockets of their owners, and sent into the fields to hunt for rodents. It has also been documented that weavers in the clothing mills used them, in attempts to control vermin population in the factories. Jokingly is had been said that the Yorkies fine, silky coats were the ultimate product of the looms in those factories. The breed left the workforce and became a companion to European high society, which pampered them as lapdogs.

Yorkshire Terriers were originally bred from a combination of working terriers; and there are varying accounts of its development. It is believed to have derived its long coat and blue coloring from the Waterside Terrier (also known as the Otter Terrier), Clydesdale, Old English Terrier, and perhaps the Skye Terriers, and then its coat color pattern is most likely from the English Black and Tan Terrier. Many people believe that maybe a Maltese Terrier was crossed into the mix at some point, to produce the long coat, however considering that the Maltese is pure white in color, I find that highly doubtful, still many argue this point. One of the problems of getting the exact Yorkie origins is that some of the breeds that would be necessary to arrive at the final Yorkshire Terrier breed are now extinct. As certain breeds disappeared, they no doubt merged into others, in part creating another version of themselves.

The Yorkshire Terrier first made its appearance at a bench show in 1861, but was called the broken-haired Scotch Terrier, and also known as Toy Terrier. It was given the official name of Yorkshire Terrier in 1870 after the Westmoreland show. In its turn, other breeds have been created from the Yorkshire Terrier, such as the Australian Silky Terrier and the Biewer Terrier.

The Yorkshire Terrier was imported to American in 1872. The British Kennel Club recognized the Yorkshire Terrier in 1874, and the AKC (American Kennel Club) recognized the breed in 1885, appropriately placing them in the Toy Group, although they are terriers by nature.

The one fact that everyone seems to agree on is that a Yorkie named Huddersfield Ben, who was born in Yorkshire in 1865, is recognized as the father of the breed, and was bred by a Mr. Eastwood and owned by Mr. Foster. George Earl painted this wonderful dog's portrait and he was said to be one of the best stud dogs of his breed during his lifetime. He was a champion and skilled ratter, who sired many Yorkshire Terriers, and had much influence on setting the actual standard for the breed, and won many prizes in the show ring. Most of the remarkable Yorkshire Terrier dogs of the present day have one or more crosses of his blood in their pedigree.

<u>Breed Standard</u>

The following is the listing for the AKC breed standard. Please understand that this is very important information if you are planning on placing your dog in the show ring. If you are purchasing a Yorkshire Terrier for a pet, the following may not be quite as important to you. If a Yorkie doesn't completely conform to perfect breed standards in appearance, making it less than show quality, it is called pet quality. When purchased from a good breeder, there can be very little difference between a pet quality and a show quality Yorkie. A breeder is looking for puppies that match the exact AKC standards, so that they can categorize their puppy as show or pet quality. All litters, even those puppies that come from champion parents cannot always be all perfect dogs. In many cases, a pet quality puppy has a very small flaw, such as a color mark, or even something slight to the shape of it's ears, or perhaps the dog is a little too small, or too large. If you are looking strictly for just a pet, and have no plans of ever showing your Yorkie, you should consider pet quality, instead of spending the extra money for a show dog. A pet quality Yorkshire Terrier will still be a wonderful companion pet, and you will not love it any less. I would however, always insist on having the AKC registration papers regardless of your pet's quality, even if the papers are limited registration, because this is your only proof that you have purchased a purebred puppy. It's also nice to have the ability to trace your pet's lineage thru the AKC, their documentation of records are flawless.

General Appearance

The Yorkshire Terrier is a longhaired toy, whose blue and tan coat is parted on the face and from the base of the skull to the end of the tail. The hair should hang evenly and quite straight down each side of the body. The body is neat, compact, and well proportioned. The dog's high head carriage along with its confident manner should give the appearance of vigor and self-importance.

Head

The head should be small and rather flat on the top. The skull is required to be not too prominent or round, and the muzzle not too long. The bite should neither be undershot nor overshot, and the teeth sound. Scissors bite or level bite is acceptable in the breed. The nose color is black. Eyes are medium in size, and should not be too prominent. The eyes should be dark in color and sparkling with a sharp intelligent expression. The eye rims are dark. Ears should be small, V-shaped, and always carried erect, not floppy, and should not be set too far apart on the head.

Legs and Feet

The Yorkshire Terrier forelegs should be straight, with the elbows neither in nor out. The hind legs should be straight when viewed from behind, however the stifles are moderately bend when viewed from the sides. Feet are round with black toenails. The dewclaws should be removed from the hind legs shortly after birth.

Body

The Yorkshire Terrier body is well proportioned and extremely compact. The back is short, with a level back line, meaning that the height at the shoulder should be the same as the rump. You should not see a humpback or a dip down in the back.

Tail

The tail should be docked to a medium length and carried slightly higher than the flat level of the back.

Desired Coat

The quality, texture and quantity of the coat are of prime importance in this breed. Hair should be glossy, fine and silky in texture. The coat on the body is moderately long and perfectly straight. The dog should have no waves in his coat. It can be trimmed to floor length to give ease of movement and a neater appearance. The fall on the head is long, and should be tied with one bow in the center of the head, or can be parted in the middle and tied with two bows. Hair on the muzzle is very long. The hair should be trimmed short on the tips of the ears, and may also be trimmed on the feet to give a neater appearance.

Puppies are born black and tan and their colors will change as they mature. The color of hair on the body and richness of tan on the head and legs are of prime importance in the adult dog. The adult dogs black should have changed to blue, which is a dark steel blue color, not a silver color, and it should not be mingled with fawn, bronzy or any black hairs. The blue extends over the body from the back of the neck to root of the tail. Hair on the tail is usually a darker blue, especially at the tip of the tail. All the tan hair should be darker at the roots than in the middle, shading to still lighter than at the tips. There should never be sooty or black hair intermingled with any of the tan hair. The hair on the head should be rich golden tan, deeper in color at the sides of the head, at ear roots, and also on the muzzle. The tan color should not extend down the back of the neck. The hair color on the chest and legs should be rich tan, not extending above the elbow on the forelegs, or above the stifle on the hind legs. It is acceptable for the dog to have a small white spot on the fore chest, but it should not exceed 1 inch in size.

Weight

The dog should be between 4 and 7 pounds, and must not exceed that weight.

The Teacup Yorkie

This is a term that is becoming more and more common, and as a former breeder I must admit that I am guilty of using the term. As far as breed standards, there is not a separate breed called a Teacup Yorkie. Many breeders advertise their Yorkies as Teacups because they are so small they would fit into a teacup, which is how they got this nickname. I have to tell you in all honesty that many Yorkies smaller than breed standards of 4 - 7 pounds are usually not very healthy, and are often diagnosed with Liver Shunt. A liver shunt is a blood vessel that carries blood around the liver instead of through it. Liver Shunts are often hereditary, and require costly surgery, and is sadly often fatal. So what are you really buying when you get "a teacup"? In some cases you are merely getting the runt of the litter. The puppy could be a premature puppy or it could be small because of the genetics in the parent's background. When I was breeding Yorkies full-time, I sold my "runts" or for the purposes here "teacups" for less money or gave them away to a loving adult only home that could offer them the tender care that they needed, because I couldn't in clear conscious guarantee their health. Understand that "teacups" aren't worth more money because they are so tiny, they are worth less, because of the health problems they will face, the future vet bills they will incur, and also they will not live as long as their full sized brothers and sisters. There are breeders that specialize in "teacups", who have studied the genetics and the pedigrees of their stock, and are breeding smaller yorkies to even smaller yorkies to create these tiny puppies on purpose. If you decide that you don't want a dog that fits the standard Yorkshire Terrier, and would prefer one of these tiny teacup yorkies you should be aware of a few things. Since the dogs are so tiny they don't have the reserve that a larger dog has, therefore if your dog gets sick it is critical that you take it to the vet immediately, as they will dehydrate quickly. Also the smaller Yorkshire Terriers are more susceptible to hypoglycemia (low blood sugar) shock, which is already a factor for this toy breed. Teacup Yorkies often need to have their baby teeth removed by a professional, as they just don't seem to want to come out on their own, often effecting the adult teeth that are attempting to come in. Lastly, one more word of caution, they are more likely to be stepped on, sat on, or injured by rough play. The breed was truly never intended to be breed this small. Although Yorkies are extremely adorable when this tiny, please think long and hard before you purchase one considered to be a "teacup" size.

<u>Where to Purchase a Yorkshire Terrier Puppy</u>

I always recommend that you purchase your puppy from a private breeder and not a pet store. Pet stores purchase their puppies from puppy mills, and usually have little or no background history of the dogs. It is very unlikely that the puppy's parents were screened for genetic problems that are passed from generation to generation. Most pet shops would like you to believe that since their puppy is registered by the AKC this guarantees the puppy will be healthy. This is not so, the only thing that AKC papers certify is that the puppy is a purebred. Even this can be falsified, as some puppy mills register more puppies than are actually born in each litter to receive extra registration slips to pass out with puppies that came from parents without papers. These puppy mills are in the business to make money; they care little about the breed. The parents of your puppy may be unhealthy or carriers of crippling or deadly health defects which may have been passed to their babies.

You have seen specimens of Yorkies in pictures, but this does not guarantee that your puppy will fit the breed standard just because it has papers. You do not know if the parents fit the standard either, and cannot see the faults that each parent has when purchasing from a pet store. A good home breeder will gladly show you the mother, and the father (if she owns the stud) and will be willing to discuss the faults and strengths of each of her dogs. Make sure that the mother appears healthy, and hasn't had any post delivery complications, which would mean she didn't care for her puppies and feed them with the proper nutrition. Ask for the medical history of the sires (puppy's father) and dams (puppy's mother).

The puppy that you are buying from a pet store has most likely spent most of its life in a cage. Many pet store puppies have never seen carpet, grass or dirt. Due to the conditions that these puppies are kept in the stores, they have been forced to eliminate in the same area that they sleep and eat. This goes against the dog's natural instinct, but your puppy has had no choice. This habit may make housebreaking your Yorkshire Terrier much more difficult. A good breeder keeps the puppy area very clean and makes sure the puppy has a separate elimination area. By the time your puppy is ready to go to their new home, it should be on its way to being house trained.

Pups from stores have not been socialized in the same way either, and you will find many of them pull away or simply ignore the hands poking thru the cage that are attempting to pet them. They do not have the same desire or need for human contact, because it is something new or unknown to them. Home breeders handle their puppies more; often giving them tender loving care, and affection everyday. Since their puppies have been handled lovingly, they are used to the touch, and scent of humans, and understand that it is good. A pet store puppy may have not been in a house before, and everything will be new and scary for them. The sounds of the vacuum cleaner, children playing, the telephone ringing, television, and video games, can all be terrifying to these puppies. Good breeders have their puppies living in their homes with them, not in outside kennels.

Most responsible breeders have also evaluated the temperament of each puppy, and they know which puppies are dominant and which are shy, which is the most energetic, and which is the most passive. Then the breeder can match the puppy to the new owner, making sure that energetic pups go to active families, and the shy ones go to a home that is quieter.

Not all home breeders are good ones either. A good ethical breeder will not cut corners to save a few dollars, their dogs and puppies all see the veterinarian on a regular basis. They know nutrition and make sure that the moms and puppies get the best quality foods and supplements available.

A good breeder will provide you with the name and phone number of their own Veterinarian, because they have nothing to hide. If you are having trouble finding a good Yorkie breeder, call around to the local vet's offices because a good breeder is often recommended to future puppy owners by a vet. You can find a breeder at AKC dog shows, usually showing their own Yorkshire Terriers. I don't have any problems with calling ads in local newspapers for a puppy, as most of them usually come from wonderful homes, but do your homework. Do not be afraid to ask the breeder questions, they should welcome them and be willing to answer them without annoyance. Remember there is no such thing as a stupid question, if you don't know the answer, then you need to ask it.

All Yorkie puppies should have had their dewclaws removed and their tails docked within 3 days of being born. If this hasn't been done than the breeder is just looking to cut corners and costs. You want to purchase a puppy that has been examined by a veterinarian, has had its shots, and been de-wormed, ask for proof of these things. Each state has different laws and requirements, you should inquire about the laws in your area, and know exactly what the breeder must provide to you. As an example of that, I live in Florida, a state that requires from the breeder to the new owner, a veterinarian signed health certificate, at the time of the puppy sale.

Ask the breeder if they ship their puppies. If the breeder says, yes, run away from them. A breeder, who would ship a puppy alone, is in this for the money and doesn't care about the puppy. Puppies in the cargo department are scared and alone, some have been known to go into shock and die. Still others have gotten lost and stolen, even shipped to the wrong airport, without food or water in their cage for hours. I have heard nightmare stories of puppies freezing on a tarmac treated like a simple piece of luggage, or others that have succumbed from heat exposure. If you have a dog shipped to you, and your dog dies or becomes sick in transport, you cannot request your money back from the breeder because their obligation to you and the puppy ended when the puppy was paid for and dropped off at the airport. If you are unable to locate a local breeder, and must go out of state for your puppy, get in the car, drive and pickup your puppy in person, or get on a plane, and fly back with the puppy on your lap.

There are breeders that will sell Yorkie puppies as young as 8 weeks old, but I don't feel they are ready to be separated from their mother and siblings, and I personally never sent them home to their new families until 10 to 12 weeks old. Separation from their mother at too young an age makes for an insecure puppy.

Another sign of a good breeder is, while you are interviewing them, they should be interviewing you. A good breeder wants to know what kind of home her puppy is going to live in, and how it will be cared for. I didn't breed Yorkies for the money, and I have turned down people when I didn't want my puppies living in their homes. One story that comes to mind is a man probably in his late 50's. He told me on the phone that he had a Yorkshire puppy but it passed away after one month's time, but he had no idea why the puppy died, and he wanted to replace it. He cursed the store he had purchased it from because they would not give him a refund. After he came to my house, and picked out a puppy, we naturally started to ask each other questions. He told me that the puppy he "lost" had been living in his garage, as he didn't believe dogs had a place inside the home. Since we live in Florida, I asked if his garage was air-conditioned and he replied no. I explained to him that in my opinion the reason his puppy most likely died was from head stroke, because a Florida garage gets very hot during the summer months. I told the stubborn man that he could not allow a dog to live in those terrible conditions. He argued with me that I was wrong, and stated he would be putting the new puppy into the same environment where the other puppy had recently died, which was his business, and not mine. Needless to say, he left my home without a puppy, as I refused to sell him one, and we had an exchange of some heated words. I did go one step further, and called another Yorkshire Terrier breeder in the area I had become friends with, to warn her about this man, she would refuse to sell him a puppy also. I hope that he wasn't able to purchase another puppy; heat stroke is a terrible death for one to suffer.

Buying a purebred Yorkshire Terrier is not just about your hard earned money, also your love and emotions are at stake, so please make sure you are buying from a breeder that truly cares about the dogs and isn't in it for just the love of money.

Before You Bring Your Puppy Home

You have found your Yorkie puppy, and placed a deposit on it. Now is the time to ready the house so you can bring him/her home. All the fun and excitement begins but there are a few things you need to know. You must remember that puppies are just like little children, they are curious and love to snoop around, often getting into everything just to discover what it is. You want your puppy's environment to be safe and secure, and if you do it correctly, your puppy will adjust quicker, learn faster, and in turn you will have less stress, so you'll be able to enjoy your new bundle of joy.

You will first need to purchase the exact same puppy food that the breeder was feeding, please resist from making any changes to your puppies diet for at least one month. Your puppy will also require, two dishes, one for food, one for water, a harness and a leash. I don't recommend that you use a collar on a young Yorkie; they can get it lodged on something and easily hang themselves. Also a collar can cause collapsed trachea in a Yorkie, more about that later in the book. My Yorkies only wear a dog harness when they are going outside on the leash; otherwise they don't have it on in the house at all. The harness should also have identification tags. Since Yorkshire Terriers have a natural tendency to track and chase, you will always want to keep them on a leash for their own safety, this is not a breed that you will train to walk beside you unleashed, without risking it taking off, and they can ran faster than you might think.

Please purchase a small bottle of Karo light corn syrup, and always keep it in the house, it is a lifesaver. I will explain the use for this later on in the book, under medical problems.

Other items you are going to need are, a good quality brush, metal comb, puppy shampoo and conditioner, a soft small blanket, kennel or a cage, a doggie bed, and a few puppy toys. I highly recommend that you invest is a good doggie gate, you don't want to ever give a brand new puppy full run of the house, it's too overwhelming especially for the little ones. Care needs to be given around stairs, a young Yorkie puppy, cannot go up and down stairs by itself, this will be something you must teach it, while supervising, so place a doggie gate in front of staircases. Another safe place to put a new puppy is in an old child's playpen, if you have one sitting around or can pick one up at a garage sale, they make the perfect safe environment for your new Yorkie puppy when you aren't able to keep an eye on them. Things in your home that you would never think about can be a danger to a tiny Yorkie, such as a door closed too quickly, and recliner chairs, so before you do anything, you must always check to see where your puppy is located.

Please walk thru your house before bringing your puppy home to check for the following things listed here. Chances are that your puppy will be a little mischievous and manage to find something to get into eventually, but the things listed here can make your puppy sick or could even be fatal. Make sure that all chemicals are stored away where your Yorkie is unable to get to them; this includes household cleaners, bleach, insecticide, pesticide, herbicide, and antifreeze.

All inside houseplants should be removed from the floor. Most people don't realize that puppies will eat the leaves and become ill. Some plants including a Christmas favorite Poinsettia's are toxic to dogs.

Puppies love to chew on dangling electrical cords. Try to rearrange all cords the best that you can, placing them out of your puppies reach. It is important that you keep a close eye on your little curious Yorkie and discipline verbally if you see it is attempting to bite on electrical cords.

Check, and then double check all areas for anything that could fit into your inquisitive puppy's mouth, such as pins, pens, pencils, loose change, medication bottles, or any other possible objects of interest. A new puppy is a like a baby, they want to put everything into their mouths, especially when teething.

Children and Yorkies

Yorkshire Terriers make wonderful pets for many homes, however extra care should be given with small children. I don't recommend toy breeds to families that have children under the age of 8. Children need to understand that while these breeds are known as toys, they aren't actual toys and rough handling can injure them. Only you know if your child is ready to handle the responsibility that comes with owning a pet, but extra thought must be given when choosing a toy breed. It is heartbreaking to see one injured because it was mishandled or abused.

Yorkies adore children, and will delight in running and playing with them and live for the attention and love they receive from a child. I have heard misinformed people state that Yorkshire Terrier's are strictly for adults. These dogs are full of energy and can certainly keep up with kids. They are eager to play and get into any trouble they might find, although keep in mind that they have a mind of their own, and this feisty dog will not do anything is doesn't want to do. I raised my own daughter with a house full of Yorkies; let me assure you that Yorkshire Terriers are a wonderful family pet, as long as they are treated properly. There is nothing like the love between a child and a dog that is a bond that certainly will grow over the years, as the two grow up together.

If you have children, I would suggest setting some ground rules before bringing your adorable little puppy home. Children naturally want to pick up and hold their puppy, while there is nothing wrong with this, too much holding is no good, especially if the puppy doesn't feel completely secure in their arms. Everyone should be taught how to properly pick up, hold, and set down the puppy gently. It is best to do this while the child is sitting down, and can place the puppy comfortably on his lap. Make sure that each child learns how to do this, so that the puppy is safe and secure. Yorkies are known to be very squirmy, and dropping them, can result in major injury. I suggest that the children sit on the floor and play with the puppy on it's own level, to also avoid unnecessary handling, and the possibility of dropping the puppy. Once a Yorkie injures its back, it will never fully recover.

Children should also be taught to leave the puppy alone while it is eating. Dogs can sometimes bite when they feel their food is being threatened; however a Yorkie biting over food is a rare thing. Even though the threat of a bite is low, the puppy will eat better, and digest his food easier when it is allowed quiet time to eat, without any distractions. Children also need to understand that feeding the puppy is best left to the adults of the house, as certain food items can be toxic. Children like to share what they are eating, especially with a beloved pet, so this must be discussed with your child.

As a family you should discuss and work out schedules for who will be the responsible party taking the puppy out, especially when it's being potty trained, and who will feed and check on it's water.

Children need to be taught that although dogs can't speak, they experience pain, hunger, fear, loneliness, hurt and other emotions that humans feel. Children should be taught to NEVER pull the dog's hair, ears, or tail. Always keep close supervision with your children and your Yorkie. As your child grows and matures, so will your Yorkie, they will create special memories of times spent together.

Your Yorkshire Terrier Puppy and Other Pets

If you already have another dog in the home, obviously there will be a time of transition for both the existing pet and the new Yorkie puppy. The key is to make the first introduction to each other slowly. When you first bring the new puppy home, it is best to have the existing pet in a cage, or have another adult hold it tightly. After about 15 minutes, bring the current pet out, and hold the new puppy, allowing them to smell each other and investigate what the other one is about.

During this time, you must pay close attention to your current pet for signs of jealously. To insure that this isn't going to be a problem, give extra attention to your existing pet to help it make the adjustment, do not make the mistake of giving the new puppy all of the attention.

There is always the chance that your pets will not like each other. Sometimes the existing pet will view the new puppy as a threat. You may hear a few growls exchanged, and they will naturally determine the pecking order between them. If your existing pet is large, you will have to intervene, the larger pet needs to understand that it could injure a tiny Yorkie. Obviously dogs, closer in size are best and safest together because even during play, a larger dog could hurt a Yorkshire Terrier without meaning to do so.

It is important that until the pets are completely getting along, that they be supervised at all times. Until you are 100% certain, do not feel bad about keeping them in separate rooms, cages, or placing the new puppy safely in a playpen, so that the older pet can sniff, and see it, but not injure it. Always reassure your existing pet by giving them attention and love, and talk to your older pet while handling the new puppy, so it doesn't feel pushed out.

Both pets should have their own food and water dishes, sharing can sometimes cause problems. I have owned as many as seven Yorkies at one time, all had the full run of the household. I never had one problem when introducing a new addition or puppy into the pack. I can tell you from my experience, that Yorkies seem to know and understand their own breed, and are usually happy to have each other for company.

In my own experiences, Yorkies don't usually get along with cats, and I would use much caution when attempting to put the two together. I have a caged parrot, and my Yorkies seem to tolerate it's talking, but I know that if they had the opportunity to get a hold of it while it was out of the cage, it would be a disaster, because the Yorkshire Terrier hunting instincts would naturally take over. Expect your Yorkshire Terrier to chase and bark at any squirrel that has evaded it's territory, such as the backyard.

Potty Training Your Yorkshire Terrier

Different breeds have different levels of learning. Some breeds are very easy to train while others are very difficult. I'm not going to lie to you, Yorkies are one of the hardest breeds to housebreak, especially males. The reason males seem to be even harder to train than females is due to their natural instinct to mark their territory. If you have a unspayed female dog in the house, and bring in a unaltered male, you can expect him to be even harder to train.

Successful housebreaking takes a lot of patience. A crate serves several purposes and it is by far the easiest way to housebreak your new Yorkie. Dogs are den animals and are usually very happy and secure to go into their own crate, so that they can rest undisturbed. They will not want to relieve themselves in their own crate because it is a limited area, which is why most owners will choose to crate train their dogs. The crate itself should contain a bed, such as a soft fleece baby blanket, and it should be large enough for your dog to turn around in. Do not feed or water your Yorkie while it is in the crate. The crate is for short-term stays like a trip in the car, or while you go out to the store for an hour or so, or when you simply do not have the time to monitor your little puppy. Please do not make the mistake of thinking that you can keep your Yorkie in a crate while you go to work all day, because that is unreasonably cruel.

You must think of the using the crate as you would a playpen for a child when you cannot directly watch their every move. The crate will keep your Yorkshire Terrier from injuring itself or causing any destructive chewing on furniture or other household items.

Keep in mind that the crate should not be used as punishment, because the puppy will not understand that concept. The crate offers you the opportunity to praise your Yorkie for being good, instead of scolding it for the mess that they made for you while you were gone.

Responding afterwards to your Yorkies accident makes for bad housebreaking experience for the both of you, and it can also make your dog fear you. Never hit or punish a Yorkie to housebreak it, the dog doesn't truly understand what they are being punished for. Just like small children, a Yorkie will learn faster if it is a pleasant experience, and will not do well if all you do is yell at it. Positive training methods achieve faster results.

You must be consistent and pay attention to what your Yorkie is doing. If you do not have the time to watch your Yorkie then crate the puppy. Before crating just make sure your Yorkie goes outside and remember when you remove your Yorkie from the crate to take the puppy outside immediately, and praise it when it goes potty.

If you are training your Yorkie to go outside, the more accidents you have inside the longer it will take to train. Never give a new puppy full run of the house until it is completely housebroken, because that makes it impossible for you to watch it, and react to an accident.

You should take your Yorkie outside as soon as it wakes up in the morning, or immediately from a nap, after it eats, after you play with them, and before they go to bed or place it back into their crate. Naturally they should go out every couple of hours during the day.

Make sure that you are consistent with your method. The best secret to housebreaking any dog is to watch your dog all the time. If you can keep your dog from having accidents in the house, and catching them, you can get them outside in time, to reinforce that is the place they should go.

Never push their nose in an accident, it is a natural for them to go potty, and they do not understand why you are doing that to them, and you could make your dog afraid to go to the bathroom. I believe this is a common potty training mistake that causes some dogs to eat their own stool, to hide what they have done. As a note, I should also tell you that some dogs will also eat their own stool due to poor nutrition, therefore it is important that you feed them the proper diet, which I will discuss later in the book.

Potty training should begin the day you bring your puppy home. Pick a spot in your yard that you want your Yorkie to use as its potty area. Place your Yorkie in this area and tell it to "go potty" or some other word you would like to use (remember always use the same word, be consistent). Keep repeating the word till your Yorkie goes potty, and then praise your Yorkie.

You can also give a special reward like a small treat that they only get when they go potty outside. I give my yorkies a piece of cheerios cereal for a special reward and they love it. If you do not wait for your Yorkie to go potty, he or she will go as soon as they get in the house, which is not your objective. Always, always praise your Yorkie for doing a good job and they will do it again on command when they hear the words "go potty". You will spend a lot of time in the first couple of days waiting and hoping for the big moment, just remember if he/she does not do it outside they will do it inside.

If you see your dog going potty in the house, the key word here is "see", because this is not the same as finding potty in your house and knowing that your dog is the only one who could have done it. If the latter is the case, just clean it up and do nothing to the dog. If you catch your Yorkie in the act, move quickly, pick your puppy up and take it to its potty place. Use the phrase "go potty" or use your own phrase. Once it finishes going, then praise your Yorkie. Praising your Yorkie is the most important part, as your Yorkie wants to please you. Giving the puppy a treat will speed up the process too.

Do not rush your Yorkie when potty training, it may be cold or rainy or you may be tired, if you make this a bad experience for your Yorkie it will take considerably longer to house train. Remember puppies can tell if you are happy with them or not by how you speak and treat them.

If you take your Yorkie out at night and it will not defecate but as soon as you bring it back in the house the dog defecates, you know your dog did have to go but you did not wait long enough for them to do their business. Make sure you give your Yorkie enough time to go and do not play with the puppy at this time or let it play with anything while you are waiting for them to go potty. This is business, not playtime, and the dog will come to understand the difference.

Another method of housebreaking is to use a training pad/wee-wee pad/pee pad. Many owners of toy breeds prefer this method. You can purchase these at any local pet store or online. Look for the pads that are treated, they will attract your puppy to go on the pads. This is a very easy method if you are using an old child's playpen, by putting a blanket on one side along with food and water, and the training pad on the other side of the pen, creating two separate areas. When the dog wakes up, after every meal, after playtime, and generally every 2 or 3 hours, place the puppy on the pad, and tell it to go potty. You want to re-enforce this, and praise after the puppy goes. Then you can eventually move the pad to a place of your liking and your dog will continue to use it. If you decide to use puppy-training pads, you won't have to worry about letting your dog go outside, which is especially nice if you live in a harsh weather climate.

Showing Your Yorkshire Terrier

No matter what you have heard, dog shows are complicated and tend to be quite political. If you know that you want to enter this world, do yourself a favor and purchase your puppy from someone that lives, eats, and breeds for showing. They will be your best guide to the dog shows, and will be more than willing to help you learn the ropes, especially since you will be showing a dog that came from their direct line.

To get started in the show world, join a local kennel club, either an all breed club or a Yorkshire Terrier club, or if possible both. Your breeder should be able to give you this information on where to find these clubs locally or you can always call the AKC.

A local club can provide you with all the information you need on training classes for the show ring, and also classes for obedience and agility classes if you are interested. These classes are informative, but of course the best way to learn and get practice for the show ring, is to attend dog shows and watch, that will also give you a better understanding of what the judges and the competitors do at these shows. These clubs also offer professional dog handlers that you can hire to show your dog, while you relax and enjoy viewing the competition from a ringside seat.

When entering a show, you will be required to know all the rules. You can order and purchase a copy of the official rulebook from the AKC. Read it, re-read it, and if possible put it to memory. Understand that because you are new to the show ring, doesn't mean that you will be forgiven for breaking rules, in fact the masters will be more than willing to point out your mistakes.

Showing your dog is a thrill like no other, and the competition is rewarding. First you need to understand the different types of dog shows. First we will discuss the conformation events, the dog's overall appearance and structure, which are purely intended to evaluate the breeding stock, another induction of the dog's ability to produce quality puppies. A few simple rules to know about this type of dog show. Your dog must be registered with the AKC, has to be 6 months of age or older, and cannot be spayed or neutered.

There are three kinds of conformation dog shows, All-breed shows, Specialty shows, and Group shows. The All-breed shows have competitions for as many as 150 breeds, which you will usually see on television. The Specialty shows (a great place to start) are for a specific kind of breed, such as Yorkshire Terriers. The Group shows are for the seven groups, in the case of a Yorkie, you would be entering in the Toy Group.

In each of these kinds of shows, the judges will examine each dog, and then present awards to the dogs that are the closest to the breed's official standard. They are looking not only at appearance, but also temperament and movement. The judges will check each dog using their hands, in order to make sure that the teeth, muscles, coat, and bones all conform to the breed standard. They will watch each dog standing in profile for overall balance, and then study the gait (walk) of your dog.

Many dogs that are in competition at the conformation shows are really competing for points toward their dogs AKC championships. A dog must earn 15 points; including two majors (which are wins of three, four or five points) that have been awarded by at least three different judges, to gain the title of "AKC Champion of Record." The amount of championship points that are awarded at a dog show totally depends on the amount of males or females entered into that breed of competition on that day. Obviously, the more entries, the greater amount of points a dog can win, with the maximum number of points awarded being 5 points. Males and female dogs always compete separately within their breed and there are seven classes of competition that are offered.

The Puppy Class, which is for dogs between six to twelve months old, which have not yet received their champions.

The Twelve to Eighteen Months Class, for dogs of that age that still have not received their champions.

The Novice Class, which is for dogs six months of age or older, which haven't won any points towards their championship, or won three first prizes in the Novice Class.

The Amateur Owner Handler Class, for dogs that are at least six months of age that haven't earned their championship. As the name would suggest the dog must be handled by its official registered owner. The owner must not be a professional dog handler, AKC approved judge or an employee of a professional handler.

The Bred By Exhibitor Class is for dogs that are shown by their owner and breeder, and are not yet champions.

The American Bred Class, is for dogs that were bred and born in the U.S. and haven't earned their championship yet.

The Open Class is for any dog that is at least 6 months of age.

When the judges have completed scoring all of the above classes, and the dogs have been awarded first place in each class, they will compete again to see who is the best of the best. Once again, males and females are judged separately, and awarded "Winners Dog" for the male, and "Winners Bitch" for the female, and each will receive championship points. Those two dogs will then compete with the champions for the Best of Breed Award.

The way dog shows work is by using the process of elimination, until the last dog standing receives the Best in Show award. Only the Best of Breed Yorkie winner can advance to the group competition of Toy Group. Then the Toy Group winner will compete against the other Best of the Group winners, which are Sporting, Hound, Working, Terrier, Non-Sporting and Herding, for the coveted title of Best in Show.

There are other events at dog shows, which can also be a lot of fun, and a great way for you to train and bond with your Yorkshire Terrier. The Agility Show, features dogs running through an obstacle course, and they are judged on how fast they complete the course. Naturally courses are set up different at each of the events and will feature balance beam, teeter-totter, and hoops to jump through.

You can also place your Yorkie in the Obedience Event, which will give you the opportunity to show how well your dog has been trained. You give your dog commands, and will be judged on how well your Yorkshire Terrier listens to you.

As a note, the AKC also offers something called Junior Showmanship Class. This is for children between the ages of 9 to 18, and they are judged on how well they present their dogs to the judges.

<u>Yorkshire Terrier Teeth</u>

Yorkies are known to have problems with their teeth throughout their entire lives. A puppy will start to get baby teeth around 4 weeks of age, and will have 28 puppy teeth.

Around 4 to 6 months of age, your puppy will begin losing puppy teeth, and their permanent teeth will start to come in. Generally, you will see the incisor teeth around 4 months, the canine teeth around 5 months, an after 6 months the molars. By 10 months old, your Yorkie should have all 42 permanent adult teeth. You must remember that these are purely guidelines, as each child is different, the same goes for each puppy. As a general rule, the smaller the puppy, the longer it will take for the teeth to come in. You will want to keep a close eye on your puppy's teeth, because Yorkies are famous for having problems during this time. It is not uncommon for Yorkies puppy teeth to remain, requiring them to removed by a veterinarian. In many cases you will see the adult teeth growing behind the puppy teeth. If this is the case, the sooner you take your puppy to the vet and have them removed the better, as this will have an effect on the placement of their permanent adult teeth.

During the time of teething you can do several things to ease the pain and control your puppies chewing.

Make chicken soup ice cubes, using either homemade soup made without salt or store bought low sodium. Your puppy will enjoy the taste, and be happy to chew on them. Fill the ice cube trays only half full, so that your tiny puppy can get these cubes in their mouth. This will numb pain, and help loosen the baby teeth, and also help the adult teeth cut thru the gums. You can soak a rag in water, wring it out, and then pop it into the freeze, and give it to your puppy to chew on as a toy. Always discourage your puppy from biting on your arm or hand. This can become a habit, and when the teething stage is done, a puppy who was allowed to chew on you, may continue to bite and chew. Make sure that you scold your Yorkie, so that it understands biting on you is causing you pain. Then replace your hand with an object, toy, rag or ice cube to gnaw on. Remember to have patience with your puppy, because it will be experiencing pain and discomfort, and don't be surprised to see some bleeding gums. Your puppy will want to chew more during this time. There are several dog toys on the market especially designed for a teething puppy, which are made to go into a freezer, this is a small price to pay, especially if is saves shoes or furniture. It is rare to find puppy teeth, as they typically swallow them.

Good Oral hygiene is important for a Yorkshire Terrier, and must be practiced from the beginning. According to veterinarians about 80% of all dogs suffer from periodontal disease, and this breed seems to be one of the worst. You can start cleaning your puppy's teeth with a wet cloth and then graduate to a soft dog toothbrush or you can purchase a soft child size toothbrush. Most Yorkies won't like this at first, but the earlier you introduce this, the easier it will get. I recommend that you brush your dog's teeth at least several times a week, using dog toothpaste, which can be purchased at most pet stores or online. Please note that you can't use human toothpaste on your dog, as they will swallow the toothpaste and become ill, dog toothpaste is made to digest. Dogs aren't crazy about the flavor of mint, and most dog toothpastes come in flavors that they will find pleasant.

Yorkies have early tooth decay problems, it's in their breeding, but there are some things you can do to help. Have your dog's teeth professionally cleaned by your Veterinarian at least once a year. This is painless procedure, as the vet will place your dog under general anesthesia, and it's also not nearly as expensive as you would think. I have known some vets to even recommend antibacterial treatments before tooth infections happen.

Good dental care is important for your dog's health. Poor dental hygiene can lead to pain for your pet and foul smelling breathe due to tooth decay. Taking good care of your dog's teeth does not take a lot of time or effort. It's very sad to see a senior Yorkshire Terriers with only a few teeth left in it's mouth, struggling to chew food. I also recommend dental chew toys to help remove tartar build-up, which is a huge problem for this breed. I don't believe in giving Yorkies bones or rawhide chews. Bones can cause the teeth to shatter and break, and the dogs usually end up eating the rawhide chews. There are several other prospective problems with rawhide or pig ears. First the obvious that it is a choking hazard especially for a Yorkie as pieces can and will break off as they chew it. Second, the rawhide can cause major stomach irritation in Yorkies, or even a severe gastric disorder from ingesting it. Please understand that due to the fact that manufacturing of rawhide dog chews and bones is completely unregulated, you have no control as to how safe it is for your pet. There have been many reports of salmonella causing dogs to get sick, and in addition to that, dangerous chemicals have been found during the processing of them.

Teeth are also a result of the food you are feeding your dog. Your dog's teeth will not clean themselves because they are chewing kibble dog food. That is a statement the dog food companies want you to believe, you can't clean teeth by scraping them with food, they must be brushed with toothpaste. I'm not a believer in dog food at all, not kibble, moist, semi-moist or canned, but more about that later in this book.

Yorkshire Terrier Ears

Most Yorkies ears should stand on their own; by the age of 3 months, but some take longer than others. In my experience I have found that the larger the ears, the harder for them to stand. If you are lucky and have purchased from a good breeder, your puppy's ears have already been trained and are standing at attention. Some Yorkies will have ears that go up and down while they are teething; encourage your puppy to keep ears up by gently massaging them in the up position.

To help train the ears to stand, the first thing you will want to do is shave the hair off the ears, using a clipper, which will remove any extra weight on the ears. If you are afraid to do this yourself, take your Yorkie to a dog groomer, and ask them to do it for you. Massage the ears, up and into position several times a day. It is not uncommon to see a Yorkshire Terrier that holds up one ear, but flops the other one, and in this case I think it's especially important to get the weak ear to stand.

If you have a puppy that seems resistant to holding it's ears up, you will have to do something to fix them, just relax this is not the end of the world. There are several different methods for taping ears, and they all seem to work fairly well, from folding the ears at the bottom inward and taping at the base for support, to taping a heavy paper backing on the back of the ears for support. I would strongly suggest that you let someone, the Yorkie breeder, vet, or dog groomer do the ear taping for you, and allow them to also remove the tape. If this isn't done carefully and properly, you risk tearing the ear itself. Most pups' only need their ears taped for a few days, and will hold their ears in perfect placement when the tape has been removed. Still you will get a stubborn one, once in a while, who needs their ears taped two, perhaps even three times. I have never had a puppy whose ears couldn't be fixed, and with that being said, much of it has to do with the timing. If you don't get your Yorkshire Terriers ears to stand before the age of 6 months, you have missed the timeframe window, and your dog will have floppy ears forever. While you will not love your dog any less if it has floppy or proper standing ears, it will matter should you decide to show your dog or breed it later.

Adult ear care is very easy. Under normal circumstances Yorkies are not prone to ear infections as long the ears are kept clean. Since most Yorkshire Terriers go to the groomers routinely, they rarely if ever get an ear infection, although they are prone to getting wax buildup inside their ears due to a great deal of hair in the canal, which a groomer will pluck out. If you are grooming your dog at home, only a gentle cleaning should be needed. Never poke or probe the internal ear canal, do not use a cotton tipped swab. These only push dirt deeper into the ear canal, causing a serious problem. For a gentle cleaning, you can use mineral oil applied to a cotton ball, and lightly wipe the surface of the external ear.

You do want to keep an eye on your dog's ears for excessive matting of hair, waxy buildup, redness or inflammation around the ear, retention of dirt, any foreign materials or objects in the ear canal. It is also a good idea to actually smell your dog's ears, because a foul odor is often a sign of an ear infection. Keep in mind that mites, fleas, and ticks like the dark, and somewhat moist inaccessible area of the ear. If you think that your dog has a problem, consult with your veterinarian as soon as possible. In the case of a severe infection, neglecting it could result in deafness. Other telltale signs that your Yorkie is suffering from an ear problem are, excessive shaking of its head, pawing and scratching at the ears. Should you also notice your dog has a tilted head; this can be a sign that the side, which is being held down, is the painful side. Your Yorkie can't speak to you, but they do have other ways of communicating, pay attention to your dog for clues of illness.

Brushing and Bathing

A Yorkshire Terrier can be the greatest companion you will ever have, but with that love and affection comes much responsibility. Yorkie grooming is a large responsibility that must be done on a daily basis, or you will end up with a dog that is matted. One of the many reasons that Yorkies are so popular is they have hair, not fur, in fact the hair found on a Yorkie is almost identical to human hair. Yorkshire Terriers are a single coated breed, which means they do not shed. They are wonderful pets for households that have an allergy suffer, because their coat doesn't contain dander, making them hypoallergenic. If you have purchased a Yorkie then you must make the commitment to brush your dog daily. A Yorkies hair is soft and silky, but if you fail to care for it properly, it will become tangled and matted quickly. You need to brush your own hair everyday, and you will have to do the same for your Yorkie. A good brushing habit can be during the evening while you are watching TV. Your Yorkshire Terrier will naturally want to sit on your lap during this time, and will quickly come to understand and appreciate and even enjoy it's nightly brushing.

Please invest in a good quality hairbrush; you will be using it daily. You must make sure that you brush properly, starting underneath, and working towards to top, brush the hair in small sections. Be gentle, especially when you encounter a knot or small matted area, working from the bottom towards the roots. Take extra care to brush areas that are often overlooked, the neck, and belly. Never brush a Yorkie while it's coat is totally dry. I recommend that you keep a spray mist bottle with a 50/50 solution of water and a good quality human hair conditioner, and lightly mist your dog's coat before the brushing routine. After you are finished brushing, you should run a good quality metal dog comb thru the hair to check for snarls and knots that you have missed during the brushing.

If you find you don't have the time to brush your dog daily, and your Yorkshire Terrier becomes matted, you always have the option to shave it down into a puppy cut, and then start fresh, growing the hair back again. You would be surprised at how quickly their coat grows. You want to avoid major matting, because this becomes painful for your dog pulling on their skin.

If you are planning on having your Yorkie puppy grow out into a full show coat, the sooner you introduce a hair bow the better. You can expect that the puppy will manage to remove it the first few times, and you should immediately replace it when you notice that it is missing. After a month or two, your Yorkie will leave its hair bow in place finally accepting it as being normal. Take care not to make the rubber band on the hair bow too tight; your dog's eyes shouldn't be bulging from its head, it shouldn't be uncomfortable for your Yorkie to wear. A hair bow not only gives a neat and pretty appearance, it also has the purpose of keeping the dog's hair out of its eyes.

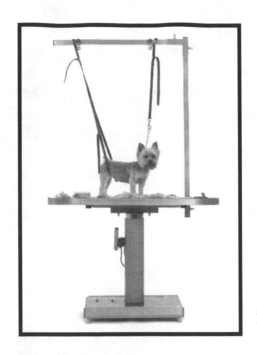

Grooming

A Yorkshire Terrier should be bathed and groomed at least once a month. The length of the coat and the quality of your Yorkies coat will most likely influence how often your dog needs to be groomed professionally. If your Yorkie has a soft coat or a dark cottony coat you will find that it is much harder to maintain than a high quality silky coat. I usually recommend that if your dog has a poor quality cottony coat to keep it in a shorter puppy cut for easier maintenance because this type of coat mats badly. If you decide you want your dog in a long show coat it will require much more work, and a bath twice a month. Male Yorkies are more work than females, because you may need to "spot wash" with a damp washcloth and warm water, the side of the body of a male dog, where he is likely to have urinated on his own long hair daily.

Naturally if your dog plays outside and gets dirty, you'll need to bathe it more frequently and I would suggest keeping it with a short puppy haircut. I give my Yorkies their bathes in the kitchen sink using the sprayer nozzle, and I find they are easier to handle rather than leaning over a bathtub.

Most Yorkshire Terrier owners take their dogs to a professional groomer once a month. A groomer will give your Yorkie a bath, trim the nails, trim the hair on the ears, around the anus, between the pads of the paws, and in some cases around the eyes. Also the groomer will trim your Yorkies nails, this must be done with care to avoid cutting the quick, which contains nerves and blood vessels. If this quick is accidentally cut, the nail will bleed requiring a styptic powder to stop it, don't ever trim your dog's nails without first having this on hand. A groomer should express your dog's anal glands, which is one of the unpleasant aspects of being a dog groomer. The reason dogs have these glands are, when a dog passes a stool, pressure is placed on the glands which are located on either side of the anus, and these glands secrete a fluid along with the stool. Every dog has a different odor to their secretion in order to identify him, which is one of the reasons dogs will sniff each other's behinds. On rare occasions, a dog's anal glands will become impacted, and Yorkies are one of the breeds that can have this problem. The signs of impacted anal glands are, dragging their butt on the floor often called scooting, tail chasing, swollen anus, and excessive licking or biting of the tail or anus area.

The sooner your puppy goes to the groomer the better they will be about it. Make sure you locate a good groomer, make phone calls, and don't be afraid to ask them questions. The shop should be clean, and you should be able to see them working on dogs when you enter. If they have something to hide, and you aren't able to view the working area, which is in the back for employees only, take your dog and leave. Make sure the groomer that will be handling your tiny Yorkie will do so gently, and carefully. If you have the opportunity to observe them working on a dog, watch their manner, and see if they talk and reassure the dog they are working on.

You need to take several things into consideration before trusting your Yorkshire Terrier with a complete stranger. Grooming is often a stressful time for your dog, so finding the correct groomer will be helpful, and your dog will develop a relationship with them.

The best way to find a good groomer is to ask around at the dog clubs or shows. Another option is to check with the dog groomer associations, because if a groomer is a member you have a better chance that he is reputable. Make sure that the groomer has the proper certification in your state and is licensed. Some groomers do certain breeds better than others, look for someone that has a large Yorkshire Terrier clientele base. If you aren't happy with the first haircut, find someone else; it may take you several groomers before you find the right one. You can expect your dog will be in their care for several hours, but when you pick them up, you'll receive a fresh smelling, silky feeling, happy dog, and one that is happy to see their owner has returned.

Praise your dog when you return home with it. I tell my Yorkies how pretty they look and make a big fuss over them remember Yorkies love attention. If you make going to the groomer a happy, positive, rewarding time for your Yorkshire Terrier, it will be eager to get into the car and go the next time.

Hair Wrapping

I'm sure hair wrapping seems strange to someone that doesn't show Yorkshire Terriers, but I promise you it is necessary. This is done to protect the Yorkies coat and keep the hair from breaking off at the ends. When showing a Yorkshire Terrier it is imperative that their coats be kept in perfect condition for the show ring. Wrapping helps to keep them from damaging their coats by everyday living. If you start wrapping as soon as the hair is long enough to get around paper, the dog will become accustomed to it and learn not to bother the wraps or tear them out. The wraps themselves do not seem to hamper the dog's movement in anyway with proper placement and I promise you it does not hurt them. If you are never going to show your dog, than you will probably never have a need to do this.

If showing a Yorkshire Terrier it is a good idea to keep the coat oiled at all times. The oil keeps the hair coated and protected, enriches it with vitamins and also prevents snarling and matting.

Although, wrapping looks hard, once you have done it a few times, you'll be able to do it rather quickly. If you have rolled someone's hair in curlers than you can do this, the only difference is, you aren't rolling round; you are creating flat packets instead. Obviously you want to section the hair, the longer the hair to be wrapped, the smaller the sections should be, practice makes perfect. You'll need rubber bands and rice paper, which can be purchased at any human beauty supply store. Oil for the hair can be purchased online from a pet supply company or in a large pet store that carries specialty items.

There is another purpose for hair wrapping, it is also wonderful when your female is having puppies. The mother's long hair is dangerous to the puppies, as they can get caught and hang themselves in it, during the birth, and afterwards while nursing. Needless to say, having the hair up and out of the way, is much easier for the breeder who is assisting with the whelping process.

Immunizations

I'm going to give you a basic immunization schedule, however, many vets follow their own, depending on your location, and your Yorkies need, because certain diseases are a greater risk in some areas than in others.

The most common puppy immunization schedule covers the most essential shots. Your puppy will need 3 sets of vaccinations and one rabies shot to be protected for the first year of life. Then you can follow with annual boosters, however, be careful that you don't over-vaccinate, you must keep careful records. At least one or two of these shots should have been done by the breeders vet before the purchase, make sure you have the paperwork on those when you pick up your puppy, so that you don't duplicate these shots.

Puppy Shots

6 – 8 weeks   DHLPP & Corona
11-12 weeks   DHLPP & Corona
15-16 weeks   DHLPP & Corona
16 weeks   Rabies

The DHLPP shot is a combination that covers, distemper, hepatitis, leptospirosis, parainfluenza, bordetella and parvovirus.

Distemper... an airborne viral disease of the lungs, intestines and brain
Hepatitis... a viral disease of the liver
Leptospirosis... a bacterial disease of the urinary tract
Parainfluenza... infectious bronchitis
Parvovirus... a viral disease of the intestines
Rabies... a viral disease fatal to humans and other animals
Bordetella Bronchiseptica is a bacterial agent that causes the respiratory disease, kennel cough.
Corona... a viral disease of the intestines

Adult Dogs (after 1 year)

DHLPP... Yearly
Rabies... Every three years (after 2nd shot)
Bordetella

Remember that vaccinations for your Yorkshire Terriers health are the best kind of medicine because prevention is easier and better than the cure to these diseases. Many of these diseases can be fatal so it is impreative that you follow a vaccination program carefully. There are other vaccinations available for prevention of Lyme disease which you should discuss with your vet, depending on the risk assessment of your area. You should address any concerns or questions about these shots with your vet. The only mandatory vaccination in the United States for dogs is the rabies one, but I believe that it is a foolish risk to take, not to do the others.

In case you are wondering how vaccinations work they mimic the process of the disease. A weakened form of the virus is injected into the body, and the immune system is triggered into producing antibodies to protect the body against the disease. The body then remembers the virus and will respond to any future exposure to it and finally more appropriate antibodies get produced.

Puppies are especially at risk from various diseases as their immunity is so low. Puppies receive immunity from certain diseases from their mother before weaning, if she has been vaccinated. After weaning, when puppies are eating on their own they need to be vaccinated as soon as possible. Canine Parvovirus is particularly deadly to young puppies. The above info on creating a Dog Vaccination Plan and schedule with a Veterinary Surgeon will help to ensure the safety of your puppy. It is essential that you be provided with a vaccination history when you purchase a puppy. It is common for puppies to have worms so a basic wormer for Roundworms and Hookworms is recommended with the first vaccinations. I would expect that your breeder has already had the puppy de-wormed at least once.

<u>Pet Health Insurance</u>

Most pet health insurance policies typically do not cover routine health care, examinations and vaccinations, but this also serves the purpose of keeping premiums very low. Pet health insurance is generally used for catastrophic, expensive and unexpected events. Advanced and emergency veterinary care can be very expensive. Pets with serious injuries or illness are commonly put down because of lack of funds to save them, but with this insurance you will never have to worry about, that heartbreaking decision. The advancement of veterinary medicine has largely kept pace with human medicine, however, so has the costs. As a pet owner, you now have more options, and treatment plans available, such as cardiac surgery, MRI, CT and ultrasound imaging.

Dogs are living longer than they have in the past because many fatal diseases such as distemper have been virtually eliminated with vaccinations. Adding more years to your pet's life is great, but you need to plan for the conditions that old age presents. You can better help your Yorkie, and make informed decisions about its health when you aren't stressing out over the cost of the bill.

Make sure that you research and shop around for your pet health insurance policy. You will want to look for a company that issues reimbursement based on the actual vet bill. Many pet insurance companies utilize outdated benefit schedules; that haven't kept up with the cost of living, so make sure you know what you are getting for your money. Read all the fine print, so that it is clear about what is covered and what is not. There are several plans on the market that will allow you to sleep better at night knowing that should some unfortunate accident or illness strike your Yorkie, it will not create a financial burden on you, and you'll be able to do everything you can to save your precious pet.

<u>Yorkshire Terrier Health Concerns</u>

Overall a well-bred Yorkshire Terrier is typically a very healthy, hearty dog, especially considering their tiny size. You should make yourself aware of the health problems that are associated with this breed and learn to recognize the warning signs and symptoms. There isn't data on the percentage of Yorkies with the following ailments, and I'm not suggesting that all Yorkshire Terriers have these ailments. The Yorkies problem conditions can be inherited, congenital or acquired. If we continue research and good selective breeding practices most of these conditions will become things of the past, the breed will become stronger, and perhaps live longer. There is much currently happening in the world of research, especially when it comes to DNA mapping, and I hope that someday, we will be able to test each Yorkie being bred, in order to assure that each puppy it produces will be healthy and happy.

All breeds seem to suffer from one condition or another, as dogs are living breathing beings, therefore disease or illness can strike them at any time, just like a human. Yorkshire Terriers are lively by nature, so you will easily be able to notice when your Yorkie is sick or experiencing pain or discomfort, because the dog will automatically be less active. It is important that you contact your vet if you have any doubts about your pet's health, as hesitation with such a small breed can be fatal. Please understand that any disease will take very little time to take over and affect their tiny body, once again I will say that the smaller the Yorkie, the faster it can get into trouble. Naturally regular vet check ups play an important part in your dog's health.

Hypoglycemia is a condition that can occur in a Yorkshire Terriers and several other toy breeds. This is a condition, which causes a fast drop of blood sugar levels. This can show up as early as 4 months old, and is sometimes caused by stress, or poor nutrition, and is more common in puppies that are born smaller than average. Yorkies can get stressed fairly easily during moving to a new home, over handling, new owners and lack of sleep. As a puppy suffering from hypoglycemia you will notice a lifeless pup, shivering with chills, confused behavior, seizures, and a drop in body temperature. If you notice that the puppy's gums and tongue are blue, or gray this is a strong indication that your puppy needs immediate help and you should contact your veterinarian immediately, before your puppy goes into a coma, which could result in death. Your vet will want to draw blood or take a urinalysis in order to test sugar levels. If you do nothing but call the vet and run out the door, you may still lose your puppy, you must take action immediately. The best thing you can do is take a few drops of Karo light corn syrup and rub it on your puppy's gums, or if your Yorkie will allow it, let them lick it off your finger. This will provide them with instant sugar, and they love the taste of it. I don't recommend that you attempt to get them to eat anything in this condition, even something like Nutra-cal because they could choke on it, especially if they are showing signs of seizure activity.

This condition can also occur in adult Yorkshire Terriers from a picky eater not eating, stress such as loud noises, sepsis or complications usually bring it on from pregnancy.

Collapsed trachea can happen in several of the toy breeds including the Yorkshire Terrier. It is believed the direct cause is poor genetics. The tracheal Collapse is a narrowing of the windpipe and occurs during rapid inhalation, and excitement. The cartilage rings soften and flatten which stop the airflow to the lungs. The most obvious sign of a collapsed trachea is chronic cough, that tends to sound more like a honk, noisy and difficult breathing which will get worse after exercise. Dogs with this condition tend to snore loudly.

Yorkshire Terriers have been known to faint from loss of air, although that is in extreme cases. This condition can be easily be diagnosed by your vet using a simple X-ray. If your Yorkie suffers from this condition you will want to avoid anything that irritates them, such as cigarette smoking, perfumes, and air sprays. It is also recommended that your Yorkie stays out of extreme cold temperatures. In extreme cases the dog can be put on medications to reduce swelling in inflammation, or surgery can be performed successfully.

In my experience, when a Yorkie is suffering from a trachea attack, and the honking begins, I find that gently lifting the head towards the ceiling, and lightly massaging the neck area, seems to open the airway quicker.

Luxating Patella, which is thought to be a genetic defect. This is a condition in which the kneecap (patellar), which is normally held together by tendons and tissue, actually moves out of its normal position. A groove in the top of the femur bone allows the kneecap to slide up and down when a dog walks, but when this condition happens the ridges don't develop normally, which allows the kneecap to come out of the groove and move side to side. You will notice your Yorkie walking with one leg held off the ground when this painful condition happens, limping, or yelping in pain. The kneecap can slip out and then back in again on it's own, making the symptoms come and go which can be confusing. In the case of a luxating patella surgery is usually recommended by a veterinary specialist to correct the problem, and the dog will lead a normal pain free active life. I should add, that once you opt for surgery and fix one leg, it's possible you will end up with the problem in the other one, so be prepared, this is an expensive ordeal.

Pancreatitis is an inflammation of the pancreas. This causes the dog to have painful abdomen, and you will notice the dog hunched up. Other symptoms of this are vomiting, diarrhea, fever, lack of appetite, and in severe cases dehydration, sepsis, and heart arrhythmias. Some dogs will only have one episodes of this, and others will have ongoing problems with it, so watch their diet closely. This is usually caused by infections, metabolic disorders, eating rawhide bones, and high fat diets, and mostly happens in middle age and older dogs. If your Yorkie is showing signs of pancreatitis, see the vet immediately; not getting the proper antibiotics will result in dehydration, especially with a small Yorkie. Usually a Yorkshire Terrier will need fluid therapy, as electrolyte imbalances are common. This is easy to diagnosis using a blood test, and physical examination.

Canine Idiopathic Epilepsy is usually the diagnosis when no other known cause it found for seizures. Dogs with this will usually start to have seizures around the age of one. There are two different kids of dog epileptic seizures. A generalized seizure, which is also called a grand mal seizure, fit or convulsion, this causes an acute decrease in consciousness, repeated movements of the body. It can sometimes cause excessive salivation, vomiting, and often a loss of bladder control. These kind of seizure can last 30 seconds to a few minutes, or as long as an hour. The other type of seizure is called a Focal Motor seizure which is less dramatic and causes twitching movements in the face or limbs and will usually only last a few seconds. This kind of seizure is often unnoticeable. For both types of seizures your dog will seem restless or nervous, and start to tremble. Once the seizure begins your dog will collapse to the floor, the body will begin to convulse, and it is not uncommon for them to lock their front paws towards the face. While scary for you to witness, the seizure itself is not hurting the dog. Pick your Yorkie up, talk softly to it, pet and comfort it during the seizure. Do give your Yorkie a drop of Karo light corn syrup on the gums or tongue, to bring blood sugar levels up if they are low. Medical treatment is recommended if your dog is suffering from more than one seizure a month. Treatment will decrease the severity of seizures, but most likely will not completely eliminate them. Vets will prescribe either Phenobarbitol or Primidone, however you should know there are other options available, so make an informed decision. Both of these drugs have side effects, which include fatigue, excessive drinking, and kidney damage. There are several homeopathic herbal treatments that calm the nervous system, which I would try before the prescriptions. Passiflora incarnata (passionflower), Scuttelaria laterifolia (skullcap), Hyoscyamus, Belladonna and Cuprum Mettalicum.

Portosystemic Shunt causes the blood to bypass the liver; instead it is diverted to another blood vessel, allowing toxins to circulate through the body, which poisons the dog's heart, lungs, brain, and other organs. Normally blood carried toxins and toxic by-products of the metabolism from the stomach and intestines to the liver, where they are filtered and removed. This can be congenital or acquired. When it is congenital it will be diagnosed before the dog is a year old, and if acquired, it can occur at any age, usually caused later in life by liver disease. When caused by congenital causes, it is usually due to the Yorkie being small, such as in the case of a teacup. Signs to look for are excessive drinking, excessive urination, and loss of appetite, loss of coordination, muscle weakness, vomiting, diarrhea, and drooling. In severe cases, loss of sight, seizures, and coma can occur. A congenital shunt that is caught early is usually a good candidate for surgery.

Renal Failure is a slow deterioration of the kidneys and can be inherited or acquired, it usually happens in middle age or older dogs. The problem with Renal Failure is that the signs of it are so vague that they could mimic many other conditions, excessive drinking or urination, weight loss, loss of appetite, vomiting, and general signs that the dog isn't feeling well. This is first diagnosed with a blood test and urine sample. The main treatment is dietary. Protein, phosphorous and salt are reduced in the diet to help slow the progression of the disease. This can progress rapidly in some and slowly in others each dog is different.

Retinal Dysplasia is an irregularity of the retina of the dog's eye. This is usually inherited, however trauma to the eye or an eye infection can also cause this to develop. Some believe that it can also be caused by the herpes infection, prenatal infections that include the Parvovirus. The retina is a thin layer of tissue that covers the back of the dogs eyeball. In the case of retinal Dysplasia, the tissue is affected which causes vision problems, blind spots or complete blindness. In a mild case, the dog will show no signs of the problem, and will adjust to the small blind areas, however a vet will discover the problem during a routine examination. In severe cases you will notice your Yorkie bumps into objects, often seems confused, or stumbles while walking. Sadly we don't have any treatment for this. If your Yorkie has this condition, and the worse case happens, complete blindness, don't even think about putting the dog down. Most dogs will do very well adjusting to either partial or complete vision loss, and will use their keen sense of hearing to compensate for it.

Legg-Perthes Disease affects the hip joint and is inherited. The Yorkies hip area receives inadequate blood circulation causing the bone in the femur to weaken and collapse and the cartilage surrounding becomes cracked and malformed. Signs of this problem will show as early as 5 months old when the puppy starts to limp and is in obvious pain. Your vet will be able to make a diagnosis using an x-ray. Surgery is required to remove the damaged parts of the femoral bone. A Yorkie will usually recover well from this surgery, as the ligaments will interweave across the hip joint creating something like a false joint.

Enteropathy (PLE) which is a condition that causes the dog to lose plasma protein in the gastrointestinal tract. These nutrients are not easily replaced. This is felt to be an inherited immune mediated disease. Most Yorkies with this condition will not show signs of the disease until they are over five years of age and can be seen equally in both male and females. The most common cause of PLE is lymphangiectasia, or blockage of the lymphatic of the gastrointestinal tract. Abnormal fluid accumulation can occur. Dogs may have no clinical signs, and others may have life threatening manifestation of PLE. Signs to look for are diarrhea, anorexia, lethargy, weight loss, fluid in the abdominal cavity, edema (retaining water in the any part of the body), and respiratory problems due to the fluid accumulation. Dietary management is usually recommended, MCT oil as a source of calories, fluid therapy to correct dehydration, diuretics to remove excess fluid in the body, antibiotic therapy, anti-inflammatory drugs.

Distichia is an eyelash that arises from an abnormal spot on the eyelid of a Yorkie. Distichiae usually exit from the duct of the meibomian gland at the eyelid margin. These are usually multiple and more than one arises from the duct. This can affect either the upper or the lower eyelid and in most cases is found to be bilateral. The lower eyelids of these Yorkshire Terrier's usually have no eyelashes at all. This will commonly cause no symptoms because the lashes are soft, but in extreme cases, they will irritate the eye and cause tearing, inflammation, and squinting, which can create corneal ulcers and scarring. Treatment options are usually surgery.

Cataracts are one of the most common problems affecting the eyes of a Yorkie, and tend to develop in their old age. There are many different forms and causes of cataract formation. The only current treatment option is surgery, removal of the lens.

There is some good news. Yorkies may be prone to any of the above diseases, but this doesn't mean that your Yorkie will ever develop any of them. I have listed the above to educate you on these diseases, so that you will be aware of the warning signs, and hopefully you will never need to know any of that information. The Yorkshire Terrier does have an expected lifespan of up to 16 years when it is raised in a positive environment, so you can certainly expect to enjoy your Yorkie for a long time Please note that extremely under sized Yorkies, often referred to as teacups, 3 pounds or less, generally have a shorter life span.

Feeding Your Yorkshire Terrier

Feeding a Yorkshire Terrier the proper well-balanced diet is important, which will give your dog a happier, longer, healthier life. Due to improper nutrition, dogs can suffer from vomiting, belching, loose stools; gassiness and stomach ache after meals. More severe problems include changes in heart rate, electrolyte imbalances, seizures, poisoning, and death. To give your Yorkie a healthy life, you need to be conscientious about what you feed him. If you are "what you eat", then the same holds for your dog. All of the ads for the different dog foods on the market have left many dog owners confused, because of the varieties, prices, and claims each of them make. Yorkies seem to suffer from intestinal disorders, itching, allergies, and seizures, which in my opinion are usually caused directly by what they are eating. These problems usually start internally.

As a responsible Yorkie owner, I know that you will want to provide your pet with meals that contain proteins, carbohydrates, fatty acids, vitamins, and minerals, and I just don't believe that you can get all of that in a commercial bag of dog food. Believe it or not, some of the highest priced dog foods aren't much better than the cheaper ones; and in good conscience I couldn't recommend any of them. It would be easy for me to endorse one of these companies, and sit back and collect money from them, but I can't, I love dogs too much.

I believe in a complete homemade diet, especially for a toy breed such as a Yorkie. Home-cooked food can do wonders for the dog, it's teeth, and hair coat, and I promise you results that you will noticeably see. Cooking for your Yorkie is well worth the time and effort.

Commercial dog foods can contain preservatives, additives, artificial colors and favors, residues of pesticides, toxic chemicals, filler ingredients, waste, restaurant grease, moldy grains, and low-grade meats, which can seriously have an adverse affect on your Yorkies health. There have been several dog food recalls due to these problems, more than most people are even aware of. You will end up paying more money for these dog foods, than it will ever cost you to feed your Yorkshire Terrier by cooking for it. It is important that you feed your Yorkie a proper diet, and know by memory the foods that your dog should eat, and should never eat. Since Yorkies are so tiny in size, chemicals and toxins have a severe reaction on them, and to their health. I personally blame commercial dog food for being the direct cause of seizures in my own Yorkies. All seizures completely stopped when I fed them a homemade diet, which I believe proves my case for cooking homemade food. Although I would love to go into details here about a complete homemade food diet, the space allotted here for this book will not allow it. I wrote a book several years ago, called ***"Woofing it Down"***, which is the complete quick and easy guide to making healthy dog food at home. This book will give you lists on the foods you should feed your dog, and lists of foods that you should never feed your dog. It has over 50 easy recipes, including meals, healthy treats, cakes and dog ice cream, that are easy to make. If you follow my directions, you will only need to cook for your Yorkie once or twice a month, freezing their meals. I have heard from many people that purchased the book, followed the diet and told me how their dog's chronic illness improved after being fed a healthy homemade diet of fresh foods.

Please understand that you cannot make an instant change to your Yorkie puppies diet, they are extremely sensitive to change, which can cause stress, and turn into Hypoglycemia. What I recommend you doing is start off feeding the food your puppy was eating when you purchased it. Gradually make the change from commercial dog food to homemade food by mixing them together, each week adding more homemade food, and less commercial dog food, until after a few weeks you have weaned your puppy off of that stuff, and it is only eating homemade food.

I want to be clear with you that I am not using this book as an avenue to sell my other book. Woofing it Down, has had strong sales, and has even been picked up, and translated into Portuguese to be sold in Brazil and other countries. Although I don't have the room to go into the details that you will need to feed a complete homemade diet here, I do want to at least give you enough information to get you started. Below you will find one meal recipe, and one treat recipe. A also recommend that your Yorkie take a daily vitamin supplement, and add a few drops of omega fish oil.

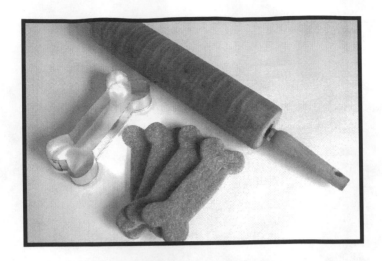

Doggie Meatloaf

Ingredients:

    2 pounds of Ground Beef (you can make this using ground turkey, or ground chicken)

    2 cups of string beans

    2 cups of corn meal

    1 cup of oatmeal

    2 teaspoons ground eggshells (finely ground into a powder)

    3 eggs

Directions:

In a large mixing bowl, mix all the ingredients together blending well. Bake at 350 degrees for about 1 hour 15 minutes. You can bake this using a few loaf pans, or you can do it the way I do it. I use a large cooking sheet that has an inch-raised side (to catch the grease run off), and shape into a nice big meatloaf; this gives you more control over how wide you want to make the meatloaf. If you decide to form one big meatloaf you may need to bake for an additional 15 minutes.

Cool and cut into slices. To serve, break the meatloaf slice into small bite size chunks with a fork. I like to wrap individual slices, put into Ziploc bags and freeze, so I always have dog food on hand.

Peanut Butter Dog Bones

Ingredients:
- 1-¼ cups of whole-wheat flour
- ½ cup quick oats oatmeal
- 1 egg
- ½ cup white flour
- ¾-powdered milk
- ¼ cup cornmeal
- 1/3-cup vegetable oil
- 3 tablespoons of unsalted natural peanut butter

Directions: Preheat oven to 350 degrees. In a large mixing bowl, mix all ingredients well. Roll out dough on a floured board and cut out shapes using cookie cutters. You can use any shape cookie cutter you want, your Yorkie doesn't care if it's in the shape of a Christmas tree. Bake on cookie sheets for 16 to 18 minutes or until dry. These should be stored in an airtight container.

Traveling With Your Yorkshire Terrier

If you are planning a vacation, you need to consider whether or not you will bring your Yorkie along. Traveling with your Yorkie can be great, if you make all the right arrangements beforehand. Poor planning can ruin your vacation, so if you think it would be best for your dog to stay home, hire a good pet sitter, or even better get a relative that knows your dog to come stay at your home, or have your Yorkie stay with them. You can also find a good kennel where you can board it. Generally Yorkies are very attached to their family, and do not like being left behind, and usually refuse to eat when left in a kennel situation, therefore unless it's a real emergency, I don't recommend it.

If you are taking your Yorkie with you, you'll need to bring a harness and leash that has current identification tags on it. This breed is one that is commonly stolen due to its monetary value, and most will go with anyone that offers them attention.

Getting to your destination by air. Canines are not cargo however; they can be considered just that by some of the airlines. Traveling in the cargo department is not a pleasant or relaxing trip

66

for your Yorkie, and I don't recommend it. Most airlines will allow you to bring a small toy dog, such as a Yorkie in a pet carrier if that carrier can fit under the seat in front of you. Make sure you ask all the details before you book your flight with any airline, and find one that allows your dog onboard with you in a carrier. I have flown with a Yorkie before, and once the plane was in the air, I pulled the carrier out from under the seat, and placed my dog on my lap. I had no complaints from any of the other passengers or even the stewardess's, as they walked down the aisles. I got a little nervous when I saw the pilot had left the cockpit and was walking towards me, until I realized that he had a smile on his face. He stopped and spoke with me about his own Yorkie, and told me that one of the stewardess's had told him how adorable mine was, and he just needed to come back and have a look at it.

If you are planning travel by car it is usually very easy on your Yorkie. The earlier your dog gets used to riding in the car, the better. Some dogs can have anxiety over riding in automobiles, because they relate it to unpleasant experiences, such as vet visits or trips to the groomers, which is why you need to make those experiences as pleasant as possible. The more positive experiences your Yorkie has riding in the car, the more likely it will be to enjoy the rides. Start taking your puppy for short; frequent car rides that end at the park, or pet store where you purchase a special treat or new toy, or another fun place like a relatives home.

You should plan on making rest stops every 3 hours, so that your Yorkie can go potty, have a drink of water, and walk around on a leash for a few minutes.

Some items that you will want to bring along in the car are, harness, leash, dog carrier with a cuddly blanket inside, dog seat belt, water bowl, treats, a few toys, dog bed, bottled water that you have kept in a small travel cooler, and food that will not spoil for your dog to eat. If you are planning on stopping in restaurants to eat, and have your Yorkie on a homemade food diet, you can ask them to prepare something simple, like a plain hamburger, no bun, and a vegetable that you know your dog enjoys. Please do not leave your Yorkie in the car unattended while you go into eat, if possible, take the dog with you in a carrier, and stow it under the table. Naturally any medication that your dog takes should also be with you.

If you are planning on staying in a hotel, make sure that you have called in advance to know that they are pet-friendly. Some hotel and motels even offer special dog beds, dog spas, and doggie day care. Most of these hotels will charge a non-refundable pet deposit upon check in, and then a daily pet fee, which is a small price to pay to have your Yorkie with you.

<u>Spaying or Neutering</u>

If you have no intentions of ever showing or breeding your Yorkie, you should spay or neuter it. Both operations lead to improved long-term health, prevent unwanted litters, and eliminate many behavior problems associated with the mating instinct.

Contrary to what many people think, having just one litter, does not improve the behavior of a female dog. The mating instinct may lead to undesirable behaviors and result in undue stress on the owner and the dog. Having a litter of Yorkie puppies involves much work, monitoring the mother's pregnancy, helping with the delivery of puppies, caring for newborn puppies, and financial expense.

During the surgical altering, a veterinarian removes the ovaries, fallopian tubes, and uterus in a female, and the testicles in the male. While both spaying and neutering are considered major surgical procedures, they are also the most common surgeries performed by vets on dogs. These operations are done painlessly while your Yorkie is comfortable under general anesthesia. After the surgery your Yorkie will experience some discomfort from the normal healing process, which should be controlled with pain medication. You will need to keep your Yorkie quiet, and calm for a few days until the incision heals.

The benefits to your female is that she will not have to experience the heat cycle, approximately every six months, which can last as long as 21 days. During this time, your Yorkshire Terrier will leave bloodstains in the house, and become anxious, possibly short-tempered and will actively seek a mate. Spaying reduces the negative behaviors that lead to owner frustration, plus early spaying of a female Yorkie helps protect it from serious health problems later in life such as uterine infections and breast cancer. Also you'll no longer have annoying or menacing suitors to contend with while she is having her cycle.

The male dog can generally be capable of breeding between 6-9 months of age. Male dogs are likely to begin marking their territories by spraying strong smelling urine on your furniture, curtains, and other places in your house. If given the slightest chance for escape from the home, to roam and search for a mate, they will take it. Some males seeking a female in heat can become aggressive and injure themselves and humans by engaging in fights. Therefore neutering a male Yorkie reduces the breeding instinct and can have a calming effect that makes them content to stay at home with their human family. Neutering also improves the male's health by reducing the risk of prostate disease, testicular cancer, and infections.

Spaying and neutering can be performed at almost any age, but it is better done early, around six months of age. Most vets recommend that a female be spayed before her first heat cycle (around 6 months of age), and a male should be neutered around 6 months to a year old.

Please understand that these procedures will have no effect on your pet's intelligence or ability to learn, or play. Most pet owners find that they have better behaving Yorkies following these operations, making them better family pets. Pets that have been spayed or neutered tend to be more gentle and affectionate, because they are less interested in other animals, and spend more time with their human family. Contrary to popular myth, having your female spayed, or your male neutered will not make it fat, because removing the ovaries or testicles does not have any affect on the dog's metabolism itself. A well balanced diet and exercise will keep your Yorkie at the proper weight, during each stage of its life. Yorkshire Terriers are rarely overweight, and will put on weight only if they are being overfed.

Fees for spaying and neutering vary from one area to another, largely depending on the economics of the veterinary hospital and community. This is a lifetime investment in your Yorkie that can solve a number of potential problems for you and your dog. Having your pet spayed or neutered is a part of responsible dog ownership, and some breeders will insist on it when they sell you a puppy.

<u>Before You Breed</u>

The only reason you should breed is to improve the breed itself. Most show exhibitors breed their Yorkshire Terriers for this reason, and when they do so they are looking for a litter of show dogs. You should never breed a Yorkshire Terrier just to have puppies for your kids to witness the miracle of life, for your Yorkie to just experience having one litter, or for the sole purpose of financial gain.

You will notice that throughout this section, I will refer to the "bitch" as female or dam. Although "bitch" is the correct technical term for a female dog, I personality find it offensive and degrading, and believe that word should be used in reference only when one is speaking about their mother-in-law.

Breeding is not an easy thing to do, and you will not have money rolling in from just allowing your dogs to do what comes naturally. There is much to learn about breeding Yorkies and I will tell you the good and the bad. I bred Yorkshire Terriers for many years, so I speak from genuine experience and have all the knowledge you seek. I admit that it was one of the most rewarding things I have ever done in my life, and I feel like each and every puppy was like a child of mine. After reading this chapter if you still decide that breeding is for you, I promise that you will gain much joy, happiness, satisfaction and wonderful memories.

Breeding Yorkies is difficult, and I will provide you will all the information that you will need. There are many things that you will need to know before you mate, also things that can happen because of breeding, and items that you must have during the birthing and afterwards, so that you will be completely prepared. Breeding your Yorkie is not risk free, every time you have a litter, you risk something happening to you pet.

Breeding Yorkies is not a moneymaking venture; in fact you will be lucky if you break even, that is the reality. The average litter size for a Yorkie is between 1 – 4 puppies. You might be thinking about all the money you will get for selling these precious puppies, but you also need to take into account the expenses that you should expect to occur. Raising a litter of Yorkshire Terrier puppies will cost money, and if you have unexpected problems, it's going to cost you even more. An example of your expenses would be stud fee (if you don't own the male), this is usually the cost of one of the puppies to be sold or pick of the litter. Whelping box, kiddie swimming pool (which I highly recommend) heating pad or heat lamp, thermometer, scissors, towels, baby scale, tweezers, baby suction bulb, hemostats, puppy milk replacement formula, puppy baby bottles, and nail clippers. Other things to take into consideration would be vet trips to have the puppies de-wormed, tails docked, dewclaws removed, and vaccinations. The mother should also be vet checked during the pregnancy and than again after giving birth. You can also expect the mother to eat up to three times what she normally eats while she is nursing the puppies.

You will occur other costs that you probably haven't even thought about. Your female should have an ultrasound the week before giving birth, so that you know how many puppies you can expect her to have. This way if you know she is having 3 puppies, and only delivers 2, you will need to take her to the vet within an hour, if the last puppy doesn't arrive. You could also have an emergency vet trip, if your female is unable to give birth, and requires a c-section or an emergency trip to save a puppy that is in danger of dying. Your female could end up with mastitis, an infection of her breast during the nursing time, and require a vet visit for antibiotics. The cost of advertising in the newspaper to sell the puppies is usually a large expense. You are probably wondering, if people aren't making money doing this, why do they breed, the only answer is because it's a labor of love. I'm not saying that it isn't possible to get lucky once in a while, and come out with a reasonable profit; I'm saying that if done properly, it's doubtful, considering how small a Yorkies litters are. If you have read the above, and still want to breed, please continue on.

Before you breed, ask yourself if your female is true show quality, has earned her championship, is free from any hereditary diseases, and mature enough to breed. If the answer is yes to all of the questions, continue on.

Do you have homes set already for the puppies before the mating or will you be able to sell them without a problem? If you aren't able to find homes for these puppies, are you able and willing to keep all of them? Are you prepared to offer the puppies buyers a lifetime guarantee for the health of the puppies (or at least one year), and are you prepared to take them back if necessary, and find another home? Will you demand that any non-show quality puppy be sold with a spay/neuter agreement? Are you prepared to fully screen each and every person that desired to purchase a puppy from you? Will you be able to part with the puppies that you have raised for the last 12 weeks and become emotionally attached to? Do you have the money you need in case of an emergency c-section, or any other complications even if this means you lose all your puppies and get no income from selling them? Are you fully prepared to spend most of the first couple of weeks of the puppy's lives without much sleep?

There are no guarantees, breeding your Yorkshire Terrier, is putting her at risk. It doesn't matter how many times you have done this, unexpected things can happen. Even the death of one pup, can be heartbreaking. You must always hope for the best, but be prepared for the worse.

It's a good idea to have someone that has done this before in your corner. You can get advice from the breeder you purchased your Yorkie from, a dog club, a breeder you have met at a dog show, or the owner of the stud you are planning to use. If it's possible to assist in the birthing of someone else's Yorkshire Terrier litter before you decide to start breed yourself, I highly recommend it. That will give you a better idea of what to expect, because if you have never assisted in the whelping of a litter before, you are going to find out that it is significantly harder and more stressful than you originally thought.

Take your time to learn and study the pedigrees of the Yorkies you have seen at the shows, this will help you chose the stud to breed your female with.

As a final note if you decide to breed your Yorkshire Terrier without the proper care, then the responsibility for a bad outcome will rest on your own shoulders.

Line Breeding & Inbreeding
& Outcrossing Breeding

There are several different methods to picking your stud, and depending on whom you talk to you, you'll get different answers about what is best. I believe what really matters are the quality of the two dogs in question, not the formula by which they are bred. The reason I say that is because commonly two puppies from the exact same litter can be completely different, one being top show quality, and the other poor pet quality you can't control nature.

Line Breeding means breeding two dogs that are relatives of each other together. Many different animal species line breed naturally. The reason many breeders will decide to line breed, is because they are planning for the set characteristics in the progeny. This is not an exact science, therefore sometimes the characteristics you wanted the puppies to inherit just don't happen, and while other recessive hidden ones do. Usually by line breeding you know what to expect. If your dog has health problems within the line, you would be further setting those health problems by line breeding, and therefore would want to avoid it. Line breeding is simply weak inbreeding, so it does still carry all the problems of both out crossing and inbreeding. I believe that the degree of the relationship does not necessarily indicate the amount of genetic material shared. Again, puppy mates from the same litters can be completely different from each other. You must pick a mate wisely based on depth of knowledge of what those pedigree lines of each mean, and what characteristics both dogs likely share, the good and the bad.

Out crossing is when you take two unrelated Yorkshire Terrier lines, and breed them together. This is risky business, because you have no idea what you are going to get with this type of breeding. You are basically breeding random pedigree Yorkshire Terrier's to each other, and will have no idea what the babies are going to look like. You may or may not get the best characteristics of the mother or the father by doing this kind of breeding, and will most likely end up with pet quality puppies. However, this is the best way to deal with some genetic problems, when you have a problem in your own line, you can do this to breed out of that problem. You do have to understand that you will never breed out of a problem completely, because it is genetic, it will still be there in the line, perhaps just hidden. Outcross should be done when you need to bring things into your line, but know that some unseen other things will accompany the traits that you desire. The best outcrosses are usually Yorkies from two separate families with similar traits. I'm sure that many out crossings wouldn't even be that if extended pedigrees were viewed, many breeds with successful bloodlines go back to each other, and will have same relatives.

Inbreeding will bring some very bad things out in your line. Things that you already know are there. The closer the breeding, the better the two dogs must be to make it work. Breeding dogs closely related is inbreeding, the point is to double up on desired line characteristics by doubling up on the genes. However, everything recessive in the family will creep up eventually by doing this if line breeding is done over generations.

Breeding Up means basically using a well-known dog to a poor quality female in hopes that the offspring will better from it. This is a bad idea, but it often happens. The outcome is nearly always the same; the owners of the new puppies will find that they aren't much better than the poor quality mother. The worst part of this is, the high quality show dog stud now has a reputation for creating poor quality pups.

Breeding Pedigrees means breeding based on their paper pedigree or breeding based solely on a famous dogs popularity or show records. One cannot take the parents show records into the ring to convince the judge of the merits of their offspring, when your dog is in the ring, it will stand on it's own merit, you cannot make your stud selection based on fame, reputation or an ad for the deciding factor in a breeding partner. Breeding must be done seeing the sire and the dam together, by their respective families when it comes to flaws, and then standing alone when it comes to what virtues they can potentially offer the other. In being honest, there is just no perfect recipe for breeding dogs, and no substitute for a well-trained experienced eye, and certainly no shame in asking for the help of someone that really knows what they are doing.

Casual breeding produces more than ¾ of all the registered pedigree dogs in the United States. It seems that everyone is breeding their own registered pet, without the serious study necessary to breed dogs well enough to avoid bad temperaments and health problems. They often do not know or understand that major genetic problems will just continue to be passed along, as they are often indiscriminately inbred. In order to be a breeder, you must get the education, be dedicated, and force yourself to be scrupulous in your selections. Breeders need to know the dogs they are using intimately. Great and consistent bloodlines have been built on good, consistent dogs bred by knowledgeable breeders. Knowledge is the key, knowing in depth what you are breeding. This means understanding the basics of inheritance, and knowing how to apply them for the best results in your breeding practices. I understand that you must learn as you go, but please read before you breed and talk to others at the shows, learn from them before you start creating lives. Any stud owner that you approach should have the knowledge to help you decide if you are making a good match.

The Mating

Most female Yorkshire Terriers will go into heat about every 6 to 7 months, beginning sometime before their first birthday. You should expect her to be in heat for approximately three weeks. You should never breed on the first heat wait until the second cycle which many consider to be the time when she has the greatest fertility.

Your female should be ready to stand and hold for the male to mount and breed her about ten to twelve days into the heat cycle. You should start counting days at the first sign of any blood discharge from the vulva. You will want to keep an eye on her attitude and temperament, and know that you could have missed a few days of a light flow. Keep in mind that every Yorkie will be a little different as far as when she will accept the male. So when you bring her to the male for breeding, don't wait until the tenth day, bring her a few days ahead of time, because she may be ready. Your Yorkie will let you know if you have the correct timing by her willingness or unwillingness to stand for the stud. If she's ready, she will pull her knobbed tail to one side, stand in front of the male, and sometimes even back into him. You will also note that when it is time to breed, her discharge will turn from a dark, bloody color to a lighter tan color. Always bring the pair together sooner than you believe is the peak of her cycle, it is better to be a few days too early than a day too late, because she will not be in heat again for another 6 months. If they don't mate on the first try, at least the two have met each other, and will do so in another day or two. I always recommend taking your female to the stud, as he will be more likely to perform in his own environment.

During the process the dogs will lock up or tie. This can last anywhere from two minutes to up to 45 minutes depending on the dog. This is the time that the male's sperm is actually being released. Make sure that you are around, some Yorkie females can panic during this time, and attempt to run, dragging the male along, which can cause serious injury to him. Most stud owners will insist on being there during the breeding, because they know that this kind of an injury can happen and end their own stud dogs breeding career. You can expect that the stud's owner will do most of the supervising during the breeding, let them do it, they have the experience, and this is part of what you are paying them to do. You will most likely be asked to calm and comfort your dog during the tie up, just pet her, and talk to her until the two break free. The pair can end up butt to butt during this process, still hooked together, just relax, this is normal and neither of them is being hurt. You will want to mate your female to the male the following day. Usually two matings are enough to allow pregnancy, certainly never more than three. If all goes well, the sperm will fertilize the eggs and the fertile eggs will migrate down the two uterine horns in search for a favorable area to attach to the lining of the uterine wall. Attachment occurs a few days after the breeding.

You don't want to over breed your dog, or you will end up with a large litter that she will not be able to carry, risking her uterus rupturing and losing your dog and all the pups. Over breeding is a common mistake that first timers make, because they are so anxious to make sure their dog gets pregnant. Yorkies are capable of getting pregnant on each and every mating session. You can have a litter of puppies from which several of them have been conceived on different days, thus this causes the puppies from the last mating to be born pre-mature. I didn't do my homework, and didn't know that this could happen. I over bred my first breeding, and my seven-pound Yorkie gave birth to seven puppies. Her belly was enormous, and I don't know how she just didn't explode. While you may think this is awesome, it wasn't. The four larger puppies were healthy and did well. Three of the puppies were tiny, and sickly. I didn't get any sleep for the first month, bottle-feeding them around the clock. Several of the pups were touch and go from minute to minute. I can tell you that all survived, but several of them had major health problems, which was expected. I was unable in good conscience to sell the smaller ones, instead I opted to find a good home for the tiniest one, and I kept two from that litter myself. You will see pictures later in the book from this litter; it was a lesson learned the hard way. In hindsight, I wonder if I did these pups any favors by forcing them to fight to stay alive those first few weeks, perhaps I should have allowed them to expire without having to suffer the fate of an unhealthy life. My dam, "Joy", also suffered from this. She lost most of her hair due to the stress of caring for this large litter, and a lot of weight. She eventually gained the weight back but never again seemed to have a good hair coat; it always seemed on the thin side. She didn't have enough milk to feed these puppies, and attempted herself to hide several of the puppies, finally orphaning then out of complete desperation to save the four stronger ones and herself. After a few weeks, she understood that I was bottle feeding and caring for the three tiny ones, and I was able to return them back to her to sleep and cuddle. She continued to kiss these puppies, once she understood that she didn't have to feed them, she was exhausted. She also ended up with mastitis, an infection of her breast but with antibiotics and she got better. This dog suffered from my ignorance, and it was then, that I knew I needed to learn everything I could about breeding Yorkshire Terriers if I dared to do it again. I studied, and learned from another Yorkie breeder and then went on to breed many successful litters, and I'm proud to say, I never lost one single puppy. My dogs had normal Yorkshire Terrier sized litters, the dams were happy and healthy and so were their offspring. While it is true that we often learn from our mistakes, I hope that by reading this book, I can spare you from making the same ones that I did. Breeding can be exciting and extremely rewarding, when it's done properly. To have the opportunity to witness the changes in newborn puppies each day, when they first open their eyes, the first wobbly steps they take, the first bark, and their first solid meal, and finally the happiness they bring to the new family they go home with are pure joy.

The Pregnancy

You won't know for a few weeks if your female has become pregnant. If it has been a successful breeding, you will notice a slight increase in her appetite. You'll start to see a slight increase in nipple size, and than naturally the next step, she will start to show. During this exciting time, you will want to increase her food intake, but you do not want to make her obese, which would lead to whelping complications. Extra calcium should be added into her diet plan; she will need it when it comes time to nurse her puppies. If you don't already have her on a daily vitamin, this would be a great time to start her on one.

The gestation time for a Yorkie is anywhere between 58-63 days, make sure you mark your calendar from the date of the first mating, and be prepared to be with her during that entire time, this means, don't leave the house!! Understand that if you bred her multiple times, you don't know for sure when her due date is. In my own experience, Yorkies seem to go around the 60 days mark, but you must be prepared for it to happen earlier.

One of my fondest memories of breeding, was placing my pregnant Yorkie on her back, and gently rubbing her mommy belly. You will see all the little bumps, and bubble movements from the puppies, its' very exciting to witness and feel such activity.

I recommend that one week before the due date, you take her to the vet for a quick sonogram or x-ray (don't worry, one single x-ray taken of full term puppies is safe). I like to know how many puppies she has inside, so that I know they have all come out, and there is no doubt when she has finished giving birth.

During this time she will appreciate more attention than usual, and towards the end, she will keep checking to make sure that you are around. I found my pregnant Yorkie liked to follow me from room to room in the house, as if she just didn't want me out of her sight for one minute. You'll also notice that your expectant mother will seem much more affectionate. You will naturally notice towards the end she is tired and requires more sleep.

The last two weeks of pregnancy you should limit some of her activities, like climbing stairs or leaping from a bed or couch. Avoid her being in extreme heat or extreme cold.

__Whelping__

Many breeders will monitor their female's temperature during the last half of the pregnancy. Some female's temperatures will drop from the normal range of 101 to 102-5 degrees to a degree or even more below normal a few hours before going into labor, however this is not always the case. From my experiences breeding Yorkies, constantly taking their temperature is not only inconvenient, it's annoying and uncomfortable to your dog, and I have had no success seeing any temperature drop that was worth noting. You will see so many other signs that she is going into labor; you don't really need to be worrying about this, the hassle just isn't worth it for me.

At least two weeks before the due date, set up the whelping box, and have your dog start to get used to it. Actual wooden whelping boxes are great for larger breed dogs, however we are talking about tiny Yorkies; therefore I myself never used one. I preferred to take a regular cardboard box, and cut out the front of it, lining it with several comfortable towels. My dog would begin to use this box, as a bed during the last two weeks. After the delivery, I transferred my puppies into a plastic child swimming pool, that contained a heating pad covered with towels, which allowed the mother to jump over the side to get in, in order to care for her newborn puppies, yet, she could easily hop out of the pool to go outside to potty and take the much needed breaks from them. The puppies were safe and secure in the swimming pool, and it was easy and sanitary to clean up after them. I do have a picture in the book of one of my litters in a pool, and you can see how well that works out.

Yorkshire Terriers in full show coat giving birth can be very dangerous. Puppies can easily hang themselves from a few strands of hair. During the time of delivery, it's almost impossible to work around the hair, and it will also get quite messy and soiled. You MUST wrap your Yorkies hair up BEFORE labor begins. Either use the method of hair wrapping, French braid it, put it up in ponytails, or cut it, but get it out of the way before labor begins. The hair will need to stay up for the next few weeks, as the puppies nurse.

Usually the first sign of labor will be her lack of interest in eating, approximately twenty-four hours before birth. You will also notice that she will lick at her vulva, and will most likely be experiencing abdominal cramping. She may scoot across the carpeting, not quite sure of what she is feeling, especially if it's a first time mommy. You will notice changes in her normal behavior, laying down one minute, and then the next running around, not sure what she really wants, extremely restless. Some females will insist that they see you in their vision at all times, afraid that they will be alone, while others may start to seek out a hiding place. I had one that decided she wanted to give birth behind my waterbed, which would have been a disaster, as I had no way of reaching her or her puppies. I was able to coax her out, using a tempting food tidbit, and then immediately blocked off her hiding burrow so she couldn't get behind the bed again. Thankfully this happened the day before she went into labor, as she started to seek out a good private place to hide. The last few days, you will want to keep a close eye on her.

When the abdominal contractions become strong, your Yorkie should be in the whelping box. You will be able to visually see her belly contracting, and feel them when placing your hand on her belly. You can expect her to hunch in the corner of the box, almost appearing that she is having a bowel movement. On rare occasions, you will get a dog that prefers to give birth while lying on her side. Next you will notice a shiny, gray or purplish bubble appear from the vulva, it almost looks like a balloon in appearance. As soon as you witness any signs of this bubble, make note of the exact time. The female will usually push out the bubble with the next few contractions. You need to be ready at this point, make sure that the sac falls onto the towels in the box, and do not allow her to run around during this process, keep her in the box. The first puppy is usually the most difficult for her to pass, usually being the largest puppy, and she may strain hard, moan or even yelp. Most will usually pant heavily as if overheated this is normal behavior. She may bite down on the towel during this, or even tear it, which helps her relieve pain; you will want to dispose of the towels in the box after the birthing process anyways. She may dig and crawl at the towels ripping them, allow her to do this. If your Yorkie doesn't pass the first puppy within one hour of seeing the water sac showing, then she is having a problem, and you need to call your veterinarian immediately, make sure you time this process.

When the pup is born, you need to quickly break and remove the sac, rub the puppy down with a dry washcloth, and get it breathing. You should NOT remove the puppy from the whelping box, it will upset the mother, instead, lean into the box, holding the puppy in front of the mother, so she can see that you are helping her, not stealing her newborn. Because Yorkie puppies are so tiny, usually between 3 and 4 ounces at birth, you don't need to use a large towel; you can carefully handle them better, with a washcloth. Most dogs will bite and break the sac, and clean their own puppy, but in the case of Yorkies they usually don't. This is a breed that wants and needs your help during the birthing process. Talk to your dog, pet her head, calm her, and reassure her that you are there with her, and everything is all right. Stay calm; as she will feed off of your emotions, if you are freaking out, she will believe something is wrong. Remember that you only have 5 minutes to get the puppy to begin breathing on it's own, otherwise brain damage will occur.

The puppy will be attached to a mass of blackish-green tissue by the umbilical cord, which is the after birth. Some believe that it is a good idea to allow the mother to eat at least one of the afterbirths as disgusting as it sounds, but I prefer to get a hold of it, and discard it quickly before she attempts it. Usually if the mother eats it, she'll end up having severe diarrhea and an upset stomach, for several days afterwards so try to avoid it. Nature tells her to eat it, to get rid of any odors or evidence in the wild that another animal could smell, telling them that she has newborns and is in a vulnerable position. You will want to use dental floss to tie off the cord about 1 inch from the puppy, and then using a clean pairs of scissors, should cut the umbilical cord. Then immediately give the puppy back to the mother, and allow her to continue licking and cleaning the new pup. You should not remove the puppy from the mother; you must do this while leaning into the whelping box. Then place the puppy on one of the mother's nipples so it can begin to nurse. While she is caring for her puppy, the process will start all over again, and she will present another pup. Please make sure that she doesn't lie down, stand on, or stomp the puppy she has, while giving birth to the next one, especially if she insists on digging into the towels. When you can grab time in between the birthing of the puppies, place each pup on one of her nipples, as you can expect them to keep falling off of them, to allow them to continue nursing. Newborns will often need assistance locating a nipple, place their mouth directly over one, and hold them on it for a minute or two until they grab on.

Every single litter my dogs have had, happened either late evening, or in the middle of the night, so you must be prepared to watch your dog. Of course, yours could decide to give birth early in the morning. If you suspect that she is beginning labor, don't even think about going to sleep, if you need to take turns with someone else to watch her, do it, otherwise the minute to close your eyes, it will be a sure guarantee she will begin labor. The entire process can take between two hours or 5 hours, depending on how many puppies she is expecting. She may have all her puppies in the first hour; having each 10 minutes apart or she may have as long as one hour between each one, all dogs are different.

If your dog is really straining, with strong contractions every few minutes and no pup is presented, get the veterinarian on the phone; she will most likely require a c-section.

You should offer her water during this process, but hold off on food. She may vomit during the delivery, quickly clean it up, and make nothing of it. Expect that your dog will have to go potty almost immediately when she has finished giving birth to the last puppy, if she has an accident in the house, don't scold her for it. She will not want to leave her puppies to go outside, but try and get her to do it, assuring her that the puppies will be fine.

Once the mess is over, and all the puppies are contently nursing, set up the swimming pool that I spoke about. Place a heating pad (on low) under a nice fluffy clean towel, and transfer each puppy over to it. Show the mom how she can hop in and out of the swimming pool to care for her puppies. She may not want you to handle them a lot, and will get very upset if you attempt to take them away from her, resist over handling them right now. Assure her that you are helping her, and not stealing her puppies, she will be very defensive and protective of her babies. The real trick is to help her, but not interfere; it's a delicate balance you will understand after your first litter.

You will naturally be excited and want to show off your babies to family and friends. Puppies can easily become sick at this time, so you need to refrain from allowing others to touch them for the first few weeks, instead let them have a peek from a distance of a few feet away.

Call your vet and make an appointment to bring your Yorkie for a check up and her puppies in the following day or the day after. This is the time to have the vet remove the puppy's dewclaws, and dock their tails; it must be done within the first three days of life. When sitting in the vet's office, people will be naturally curious and delight in seeing newborn puppies, firmly tell them that you would prefer they keep their distance from them, as they are extremely susceptible to disease at this time, and they should respect that. If they think you are being rude, too bad, they will get over it, and you'll most likely never see them again. I had one man who didn't control his large German Shepherd on his leash, and allowed it to peek it's head over the top of the cardboard box I had carefully lined with fresh towels containing my Yorkie along with her puppies. My sweet Yorkie, snapped, and bite the Shepherd hard in his snout. As far as I'm concerned, the owner of that dog got what he deserved, and I admit I was quite proud of my girl for protecting her babies, although the poor Shepherd did let out quite a yelp, but immediately backed off. Before you leave the vets office that day, you should make appointments for de-worming the puppies, and the puppy's first shots.

Caring for the Newborns

I firmly believe that all the puppies should be picked up, cuddled, held, petted, and touched each day by the breeder. This gives the puppies important socialization skills, and it begins to understand that human touch and smell is a good thing. The first three weeks will be the hardest time, and probably the most exhausting and stressful for you. If you are going to lose a puppy, it's usually during the first three critical weeks. It is important that you make sure the puppies are nursing every hour or so the first few nights and days, and that means no sleep for you. You'll need to constantly check and monitor that the mother isn't smothering her own puppies by laying down on them, or still digging thru the towels to create a comfortable place for her to lay down. Once again, let me stress here that you need to make sure that your dam's hair is in wraps so that the puppies don't get hung up in it.

The smaller pups, may need help locating a nipple the first few days, and must be placed on one, sometimes, you will need to hold a weak puppy on there. I like to make a rule to do this at least every two hours, more often if I see that the smaller puppies are extremely weak, and have thin necks, a clear sign of dehydration. The puppies that have thicker necks are the stronger ones. They should start gaining weight, a few grams each day, please use a proper puppy scale and weigh each one daily, making sure you keep track of their weight. You must weigh your puppies, record it, and watch for any puppy that's weight is going down. A puppy should double their birth weight around 10 days old.

You will want to check puppies for any signs of dehydration several times a day, to do that, lightly pinch together the skin at the back of the neck lengthwise. If it stays in a crease, the puppy is dehydrating. If the skin instantly springs back, then the puppy is thriving. Immediately place any puppy that is in danger of dehydration onto one of the mother's nipples. The ones on the bottom near the hind legs have the most milk. If your puppy is not willing to nurse, or seems to weak to nurse, you must start bottle-feeding. I like to put two drops of Karo corn syrup into the puppy formula, at this point your puppy really needs it, and I have found that it works wonders with fading puppies. You will want to use lukewarm formula, test the temperature of the formula on your wrist, just like you would do for a human baby. Puppy formula can be purchased in any pet store.

Puppies are born blind with their eyelids sealed shut. Never attempt to pull or open their eyes. By the time they are 2 weeks old, the eyelids will open, and the puppy will begin to develop vision.

Make sure that you trim puppy nails, so that they don't scratch and irritate the mother's skin and nipples. Your Yorkie should be eating more calcium in her diet, and naturally should have fresh water available all the time, do not neglect her needs, as nursing her puppies is draining her.

For the first couple of days after birth, check the mother's milk supply to make sure that she has an adequate amount for feeding the litter. If a puppy pulls on the nipple and cries out in frustration, check the milk. This can be done by gently squeezing the breasts below the nipple. Milk should flow freely! Sometimes a female will have adequate milk on the day of whelping, but the second day it will disappear, only to return on the next day. Also following

C-Sections, the milk can be really slow to come in. If the litter is small in number, be sure to check the breasts, by making sure that all are being used and emptied.

Beware of breasts that are hot to the touch and have a packed "hard" lumpy feeling. If milk is not cleared out regularly, you run the risk of an infection developing. It's a good idea to check the mother's temperature the first couple of days following whelping. Anything over 103 degrees, should be looked at with great suspicion!

Puppies: Keep clean-Keep warm. If puppies and their blankets are not kept clean, it is very easy to come down with a staph infection and diarrhea, which is serious. Puppies can go downhill quickly. It is equally serious if the puppies get chilled. Avoid drafts, etc. Even if you have them in a whelping box or swimming pool with a heating pad, you need to keep out drafts. A chilled puppy has to be warmed up.

The syndrome whereby puppies, apparently normal and healthy at birth, fail to thrive and eventually die is commonly called the fading puppy syndrome. Puppies are very vulnerable to any form of stress because of their immature immune, cardiovascular (heart) and respiratory (lungs) systems at birth. Factors such as chilling, malnutrition, congenital abnormalities, trauma and infection have consistently proven to be fatal to puppies, especially in the first 2 weeks of life when nearly 80% of puppy fatalities occur.

Enteritis and pneumonia is the two most common diseases in puppies and also responsible for most mortalities. Enteritis (infection of the intestines) is caused by various viruses and bacteria and is precipitated by poor hygiene, lack of sufficient immune protection, ingestion of too much milk, change in diet or other stress factors. The main symptom is diarrhea, which can vary from watery to mucous to hemorrhagic, followed by dehydration, emaciation, weakness and death. Low ambient temperature, a draught or a common cold (viral infection) can cause infection of the upper respiratory system. If it is allowed to progress, it can develop into a bacterial infection of the lungs (pneumonia). Symptoms include nasal discharge, rapid and difficult breathing and a moist cough. Inhalation of milk by Yorkshire Terrier puppies is quite common and can rapidly develop into a fatal pneumonia. Novice breeders are advised to make use of a vet with sufficient experience in the treatment of puppies and to always react swiftly to any signs of disease.

I like to set up towels on one side of the swimming pool, and puppy training pads on the other. As puppies take their few wobbling steps and explore, they are also starting to learn what area they should eliminate in. You can expect the puppies to play with their littermates, and sometimes be quite vocal. Your puppy will learn to bark around 3 to 4 weeks old, and the sound of their first squeaks and barks are adorable. Around 3 weeks old, you can give them a very shallow water dish, and allow them to begin lapping some water if they desire. They will be curious with the new dish addition and will most likely walk thru the water and play with it, before they drink it.

Weaning the Puppies

You can begin feeding tiny, liquidly soft food to your puppies around 4 weeks old. I usually start their first meal with a mixture of baby rice cereal and puppy formula. As they tolerate that a week later I will start them off with something simple like, cooked lamb or cooked ground beef and rice, water and some puppy milk formula and placing it in a blender, to create what I call puppy gruel, a liquidly paste consistency. One of the best ways to start feeding puppies is to give them the food in a shallow pan, like a small cookie sheet. Gently place the pups around the edge of the food, and push their face into it, they will smell it and begin to lick. I must warn you that the first few meals are quite messy, as they will usually end up walking thru the food, perhaps even roll around in it, but get the camera ready; it's also very cute. At this time, the puppies should be hopping and bouncing around the swimming pool, playing with each other. They have fully developed their sight and hearing. They should still be nursing from their mom, but will slowly become more interested in eating the new tasty food you are offering them. In a few days, when they are doing well with food, and eating three times a day, you can have mom stop nursing them.

Make sure you start to massage the ears, to get them to stand up, usually the sooner you begin doing this, the less of the chance that you will have to tape them. You will want the ears standing when future puppy owners come to visit. This is also the time to have your mother Yorkie groomed, because most buyers will want to inspect her.

When it's time to say Goodbye

This is tough chapter to write because preparing for your dog's death is a heart wrenching situation, but one that is necessary. There is never an easy way to say your final goodbyes, and the only thing that has ever provided me some peace or comfort, is to know in my heart that one day I will be reunited with all of my Yorkies, on the other side at the Rainbow Bridge.

Sadly dogs don't live as long as we would like them to, and the day will come when you and your Yorkie must part ways. We are never quite prepared for the death of a pet. Whether death is swift and unexpected or whether it comes at the end of a slow decline, we are never fully aware of what a dog has brought to our lives until our little Yorkie is gone. During the last few days of your dog's life you will want to make your pet as comfortable as possible while making the final arrangements for its burial, which will also ease some of the pain of losing your Yorkie.

You must make sure you are being realistic about your Yorkies diagnoses. If your veterinarian has given you a time frame in which you can expect a loss, than use it to your advantage by making the most of your time with your dog. You can also ease your Yorkies suffering by helping him be as comfortable as possible. Lavish your dog with extra hugs, kisses, attention, special treats, a favorite meal and naturally lots of love. While you are petting your Yorkie, talk to it, tell him how much he will be missed, because believe me they really do understand. Speak softly; don't place your own fears onto your Yorkie. The dog already knows that something is wrong, you don't want to frighten him, let your pet know that he should not be afraid, and that it is ok for him to go. You will want to keep a positive attitude while you are around your dog. Yorkies are highly sensitive animals and know when their owners are upset. Be sure and take many pictures in these last days, because you will cherish them for years to come.

Consult with your veterinarian, and don't be afraid to ask questions about treatment or care options available. It is sometimes difficult to strike a balance between your Yorkie's health and its general happiness. Sometimes, treatments for diseases or injuries can substantially lower your dog's quality of life.

It is best to decide now on the arrangements for your pet's burial, because if you know your option beforehand, you'll have one less thing on your mind when your beloved dog passes on. You can choose to bury your Yorkie at home in the yard, in a pet cemetery or have the body cremated keeping the ashes in an urn somewhere in your home. Only you can decide what is best for you. I have buried one in my backyard, with a beautiful stepping stone marker that has her name on it, and then planted a flowering bush for her over the gravesite. I also have had several of my Yorkies cremated, and their ashes were placed in sealed pink marble urns, either way, I hurt deeply and cried a river of tears for each and every one of them.

Euthanasia is by far the most difficult decision that any dog owner can face, but sometimes it really is the only humane option. If your Yorkie is suffering and your veterinarian recommends that you should put him to sleep, please listen. These are the dreaded words that no dog owner ever wants to hear during a vet visit but understand that Doctors of veterinary medicine do not exercise this option lightly. Their medical training and professional lives are dedicated to diagnosis and treatment of disease. Veterinarians are keenly aware of the balance between extending an animal's life and it's suffering. Euthanasia is the ultimate tool to mercifully end a dog's suffering. Euthanasia is the induction of painless death. In veterinary practice, it is accomplished by intravenous injection of a concentrated dose of anesthetic. The animal may feel slight discomfort when the needle tip passes through the skin, but this is no greater than for any other injection. The euthanasia solution takes only seconds to induce a total loss of consciousness. This is soon followed by respiratory depression and cardiac arrest.

Everyone secretly hopes for a pet's peaceful passing, hoping to find it lying in its favorite spot in the morning. The impact of a pet's death is significantly increased when, as responsible and loving caretakers, we decide to have the pet euthanized. It is natural to look for signs of health and see them even when they aren't really there. Often dog owner's delay performing euthanasia on their dogs because they cannot bear the thought of parting with them, we may postpone the decision, bargaining with ourselves that if we wait another day, the decision will not be necessary. While this act is highly understandable, it is also extremely unfair to their Yorkie, and quite selfish. Guilt has a way of sitting heavily on the one who must decide. The fundamental guideline is to do what is best for your dog, even if you must suffer.

There is nothing that anyone can say that will make this idea any easier, except to know that your Yorkie is no longer suffering or in pain, and this is your last act of kindness and compassion towards your pet. Doing what is best for your Yorkie, your family, and the situation is a private matter. Some individuals find the process of putting their beloved pet to sleep about as peaceful as death can possibly be, and in reality, it is the most peaceful option for most animals that are suffering or have been battling a long-term illness or disability. The number one statement of concern that most pet lovers who are considering having their honored pet put to sleep is that they need to feel sure that it is the right time. Nobody wants to watch his or her dog suffer needlessly. At the same time, nobody wants to rob his or her pet of possible active and tolerable months or even years, nor are we ever truly ready to let go. I myself have made the appointment three times before I was finally able to take my Yorkie in. This can be part of the process for some people. While this is a very difficult time for all pet owners, the absolute greatest piece of advice I have ever heard regarding the timing of putting a dog down was relatively simple but carried the weight of a thousand elephants; look into his eyes and trust your heart. While it certainly doesn't seem very scientific or medically sound, people who have a significant bond with their Yorkie are able to understand when the "light" in his eyes has deteriorated too far. If you need the scientific part, than ask yourself the following questions, and make sure that you answer them honestly.

1. Is your Yorkie's health condition prolonged, recurring or getting worse with time?
2. Is your Yorkie's condition no longer responding to medical treatment or therapy?

3. Is your Yorkie in constant pain, or suffering physically or mentally?
4. Is it impossible to lessen your Yorkie's pain or suffering?
5. If your Yorkie recovers, is he likely to be chronically ill or unable to take of himself?
6. Can I provide the necessary care?
7. Can I afford the cost of medical treatment now – or over a long period of time?
8. Is your Yorkie still eating well or has he lost considerable weight?
9. Is your Yorkie still playful and happy?
10. Is your Yorkie still affectionate towards you and others?
11. Is your Yorkie interested in activity's surrounding it?
12. Does your Yorkie seem tired and withdrawn most of the time?

The decision to perform euthanasia on your dog should not be yours alone. Talk to your vet, and of course other family members in the household. Your Yorkie is part of your family – the final choice should be a family decision.

If you are lucky, in some cases, your Yorkie will tell you it's time. He will start to separate himself from you. If he has spent nearly every night sleeping beside, or in, your bed and he seeks out places that resemble a cave, he may be preparing himself for death. Pack animals in particular have been known to separate themselves from the pack in order to prevent the strong from becoming injured while protecting the weak, therefore pay special attention to your Yorkie if it seems to be searching for a hiding spot. Whatever decision make, you know that you have acted in the best interest of your dog and that he has had a happy life with you.

The decision to be with your Yorkie during the euthanasia is a personal one. While it is a simple and quite, even peaceful procedure, there is no shame in keeping his memory as he was in life. Some people feel as though they are betraying their pet by not following through to the end, only you can decide, it's a decision you must live with, without regret, forever. If you opt not to go in with your Yorkie, the veterinary staff will be able to offer your dog absolutely everything he or she will need. There is no shame and there is no guilt necessary. I myself made the decision to be with my Yorkies during this time. I have had to make the sad decision to put down 3 of my Yorkies during the course of my lifetime so far, something I have never regretted, as it was the right thing to do with each one of them at the time. I was able to pet their heads, kiss their snouts, and whisper that I loved them in their ear as they relaxed and went to sleep. I saw them peaceful, at rest, and no longer suffering, and because I was able to be there with them at the end, it made me feel better, and I was able to see how the process worked, and knew that they had a peaceful, quiet, relaxed death. I was given comfort and sympathies from my vet and the office staff, who understood my pain and loss. The dignity and grace shown by our dying Yorkie's may well be their last gift to us.

You will grieve for your Yorkie; this is a process that will take time to get thru. For many of us who love our dogs like children, their death can affect some of us more than the death of a close relative or friend. The death of a pet leaves few people totally untouched, but there are exceptions to every rule. When a pet dies, we expect that others will acknowledge our deep pain, loss and hurt. The bond between you and your Yorkie is as valuable as any of your human relationships; but other people may not always appreciate the importance of its loss. Be prepared to encounter those that will say, "Oh it was just a dog, get over it". The process of grieving for a dog is no different than mourning the death of a human being. The difference lies in the value that is placed on your pet by you alone, and others that have suffered from the same. Seek validation for your pain from people who will understand you and ones that are willing to help you during the bereavement process, and ignore the ignorance of those that will not. Remember that you do not need anyone else's approval to mourn the loss of your Yorkie, nor do you have to justify your feelings to anyone. The joy found in the companionship of an animal is a blessing not given to everyone. Your life was and will continue to be brighter because of the special time you shared with your Yorkie. This is the best testament to the value of your pet's existence.

Yorkshire Terrier Facts, Oddities and Interesting Tidbits

The Guinness World Book of Records lists Tiny Pinocchio (nicknamed Noki) as the smallest dog in the world. Owned by Linda Skeels-Hopson, he stood 4 ½ inches tall, and weighed only one pound. Tiny Pinocchio had taken on some celebrity status making appearances on television shows Oprah, and the Today Show, sadly he died on June 1, 2004, at the tender age of 2 ½ years old.

Prior to that, in 1995, a Yorkshire Terrier named Big Boss, was listed as the smallest dog in the world, which stands 4.7 inches tall, weighs only 17 ounces and is owned by Dr. Chai Khanchanakom who recides in Thailand. Prior to 1995, they had listed a Yorkshire terrier named Thumbelina, who stood 5 ½ inches tall as the smallest dog.

Yorkshire Terriers have been owned by such famous people as, BruceWillis, Britney Spears, Justin Timberlake, Hilary Duff, Paris Hilton, Mariah Carey, Whiteney Houston, Donnie Osmond, Vanessa Williams, Tammy Faye Baker, Audrey Hepburn, Tara Reid, Heather Locklear, Ivana Trump, Stevie Nicks, Barbara Mandrell, Carmen Electra, Leonardo DiCaprio, and Kelly Clarkson to name just a few.

A Yorkshire Terrier named Pasha, lived in the White House, and was owned by Tricia Nixon.

A Yorkshire Terrier named Smoky became famous during World War II. Adopted by William Wynne of Ohio while he was serving with the 5th Air Force in the Pacific Theatre. Mr. Wynne trained smoky to perform tricks to entertain his comrades, and Smoky was entered into Yank Magazines Best Mascost contest, winning first price, landing her picture on the cover. Smoky used her small size to help run communication wire through a culvery that was under a runway. Without the assitance of this Yorkshire Terrier, the runway would have needed to be excavated while cable was being laid. Smoky was deemed the most famous dog of World War II, and returned home to Ohio with Mr. Wynne.

Famous Yorkshire Terriers include Audrey Heyburn's Yorkie 'Mr. Famous' who appeared with her in Funny Face, Chow Mien from Gypsy, Spike the former canine sidekick of Joan Rivers, and Mignon, who was Lisa Douglas' (played by Eva Gabor) Yorkshire Terrier on the television series Green Acres. Yorkies have been growing in popularity and have been recently featured in such films as "Meet the Fockers", "Urban Legend", and "Daltry Calhoun".

Toto from the original book version of L. Frank Baum's The Wonderful Wizard of Oz was illustrated as a Yorkshire Terrier. In later books of the Oz series, Toto was a Boston Terrier. In the 1939 film version, Toto was played by a Cairn Terrier, not a Yorkie.

The first Yorkshire Terrier to win Best of Show at Crufts, the world's largest dog annual dog show was in 1997, champion Ozmilion Mystification.

Some interesting Yorkie facts that you probably don't know. Yorkies do not just see in black in white, they see in color, but their perception of color is not the same as it is for people. They cannot distinguish between red, orange, yellow or green. They can see various shades of blue. When comparing dog and human vision, people are better at depth perception, color perception and seeing minute details of an object. Dogs are better at seeing in dim light, and respond to an image rapidly, detecting the slightest motion, also Yorkies have better peripheral vision than humans.

A Yorkie's sweat gland is located between its paw pad.

During the first two weeks of a Yorkie's life, it will sleep around 90% of the time, approximately 21 hours, and will nurse the other 3 hours of the day.

If never cut a Yorkshire Terrier can grow hair up to 2 feet in length.

JUST FOR FUN

So much of this book has dealt with serious subjects, and while owning a dog of any breed has its share of responsibilities, pet ownership also brings much happiness and joy. You have purchased your Yorkshire Terrier for enjoyment, and companionship, that's what dogs are all about, so relax, love and have fun with your new puppy.

YORKSHIRE TERRIER CROSSWORD PUZZLE

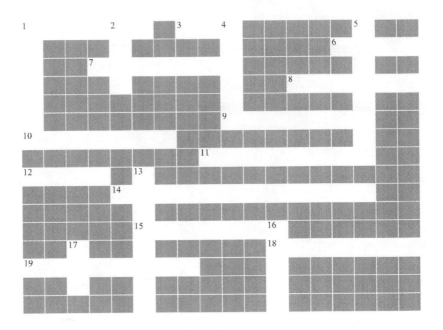

ACROSS

1. To have a female surgically altered
3. Which of the seven groups is the Yorkshire Terrier listed
6. Yorkshire Terriers have no fur, instead they have?
7. Best place to purchased a purebred puppy
8. Name used for an undersized Yorkshire Terrier
9. Country of Origin for a Yorkshire Terrier
10. Yorkshire Terriers should visit this person once a month
11. This should be done daily
12. Name for the father of the puppies
14. What do you call a doctor that cares for animals
15. Found on the top of a Yorkshire Terrier show dog
18. Attached to the topknot
19. Title earned in a dog show

DOWN

1. Common Term used when entering a dog show
2. What might have to be taped on a Yorkshire Terrier Puppy
4. Common nickname for a Yorkshire Terrier
5. They bark to announce someone at the door
13. What a puppy is doing when losing baby teeth
16. Average amount of puppies in a Yorkie litter
17. Favorite Place for a Yorkshire Terrier to sit

YORKSHIRE TERRIER WORD FIND

```
A Y C N A F D O G D G J H L A
A W A T C H D O G R J A O M X
E E R G I D E P O G I V O V Y
L P C Y A P S O N R I A T O Q
A P H Z W A M I B N F E R S O
P U A V C I S O G F E K B H C
D P M T N R W R E T S U A O V
O P P G U F E C H H Y I T W L
G Y I N E T T I I V G X H I M
E T O O U I N R R G Z Q Y N P
U O N E O G E H I U E E Q G R
E V N N P T G N I D E E R B E
A Y A C E L U F R E D N O W T
B T C G T M R E I R R E T H T
E T O P K N O T K Y O T A V Y
```

AFFECTIONATE	PET
BATH	PRETTY
BREEDING	PUPPY
CHAMPION	SHOWING
DOG	SPAY
FANCY	TEETHING
GROOMING	TERRIER
HAIRBOW	TOPKNOT
LAPDOG	TOY
LOVING	WATCHDOG
NEUTER	WONDERFUL
NURSING	YORKSHIRE
PEDIGREE	

OTHER BOOKS AVAILABLE BY THIS AUTHOR

Woofing it Down
The Quick & Easy Guide to Making Healthy Dog Food At Home

Lapping It up
The Quick & East Guide to Making Healthy Cat Food At Home

The Ultimate Yorkshire Terrier Book
Guide to Caring, Raising, Training, Breeding, Whelping, Feeding and Loving a Yorkie

Tales of the Whosawhachits
Key Holders of the Realm (Book 1 of series)
Young Adult Novel
(YABI Award Winner)

Mirror Mirror
Seven Years Bad Luck
Adult Paranormal Fantasy Novel
(Covey Award Winner)

COMING SOON

Tales of the Whosawhachits
Enter the 5th Realm (Book 2 of series)
Young Adult Novel

Pecking it Up
Recipes for feeding your Parakeet, Cockatiel, Finch, Canary, Lovebird, African Grey, Cockatoo, Conure, Dove, Lorie, Macaw, Quaker and more

True Encounters with Imaginary Friends
Young Adult Novel